T0253510

The Ultimate Guide to Functions in Power Query

Turn Raw Data into Actionable Insights

Omid Motamedisedeh

Apress®

The Ultimate Guide to Functions in Power Query: Turn Raw Data into Actionable Insights

Omid Motamedisedeh
Brisbane, QLD, Australia

ISBN-13 (pbk): 978-1-4842-9753-7 ISBN-13 (electronic): 978-1-4842-9754-4
https://doi.org/10.1007/978-1-4842-9754-4

Managing Director, Apress Media LLC: Welmoed Spahr
Acquisitions Editor: Susan McDermott
Development Editor: Laura Berendson
Editorial Project Manager: Jessica Vakili
Copy Editor: Mary Behr

Cover designed by eStudioCalamar

Cover image by Jordy from Pixabay

Distributed to the book trade worldwide by Springer Science+Business Media New York, 1 New York Plaza, Suite 4600, New York, NY 10004-1562, USA. Phone 1-800-SPRINGER, fax (201) 348-4505, e-mail orders-ny@springer-sbm.com, or visit www.springeronline.com. Apress Media, LLC is a California LLC and the sole member (owner) is Springer Science + Business Media Finance Inc (SSBM Finance Inc). SSBM Finance Inc is a **Delaware** corporation.

For information on translations, please e-mail booktranslations@springernature.com; for reprint, paperback, or audio rights, please e-mail bookpermissions@springernature.com.

Apress titles may be purchased in bulk for academic, corporate, or promotional use. eBook versions and licenses are also available for most titles. For more information, reference our Print and eBook Bulk Sales web page at www.apress.com/bulk-sales.

Any source code or other supplementary material referenced by the author in this book is available to readers on GitHub (github.com/apress). For more detailed information, please visit https://www.apress.com/gp/services/source-code.

Paper in this product is recyclable

To my dear mom and dad, in heartfelt appreciation for your invaluable support and assistance

Table of Contents

About the Author

 **Omid Motamedisedeh** is a freelance data and business intelligence analyst with a PhD in Industrial Engineering. He's currently working towards his second PhD at Queensland University of Technology. Omid is the author of several articles in industry journals (*Electric Power Systems Research, Journal of Building Engineering, Energy, Neural Computing and Applications*, and others), and seven books (all in Farsi) namely *Managing Data Entry in Excel by Data Validation, Data Analysis by Excel's Pivot Table, Power Query as The Magic of Excel, 222 Most Useful Functions in Excel 2016, Useful Excel Functions in Excel 2019, Reference of Functions in Excel 2021*, and *From Drawing Charts to Creating Dashboards in Excel 2016*.

About the Technical Reviewer

Bo Rydobon (a.k.a. Excel Wizard) is a Microsoft Excel expert and YouTuber from Thailand who is known for his speed and mastery of Excel. He is also the creator of the Excel Wizard YouTube channel, where he shares tips and tricks on how to use advanced dynamic arrays. He actively contributes on Excelforum.com and became a Top 5 reputation within a few years. His participation in the Excel BI LinkedIn Excel Challenge drew notable attention due to his impressive response. In 2022, Bo Rydobon won the Excel Esports Speedrun organized by the Financial Modeling World Cup.

Bo Rydobon is an inspiration to Excel users all over the world. He shows that anyone can learn Excel and become an expert, regardless of their background or experience.

Acknowledgments

I would like to express my sincere gratitude to the individuals who have played an indispensable role in supporting me throughout the process of writing this book. My appreciation extends to both those within my professional circle and those who hold a personal place in my life.

First and foremost, I extend heartfelt thanks to Faranak, whose unwavering belief in me and encouragement provided the catalyst for embarking on this writing journey.

I am equally grateful to Bo Rydobon, my esteemed technical reviewer, whose invaluable insights and motivating feedback have significantly enriched the quality of this work.

Furthermore, I wish to extend my thanks to the Apress team, including Susan McDermott (Editorial Director), Shobana Srinivasan (Book Coordinator), and Shaul Elson (Editorial Manager), for their commendable professionalism and collaborative approach. Their contributions have transformed working with Apress into a truly gratifying experience.

Lastly, my profound and enduring appreciation goes to Professor Hamid Reza Irani, who imparted foundational knowledge of Excel during my undergraduate years, and to Mike Girvin, a cherished Excel mentor. Mike's prolific Excel tips shared on the ExcelIsFun YouTube channel have been a wellspring of learning for all Excel fans like me.

Introduction

In today's data-driven landscape, the ability to seamlessly transform raw data into meaningful insights is a skill of paramount importance. *The Ultimate Guide to Functions in Power Query* stands as a beacon for Excel and Power BI enthusiasts, equipping them with the tools to unlock the full potential of their data manipulation endeavors.

In this comprehensive guide, you will delve into the world of Power Query functions, the building blocks that empower users to effortlessly manipulate, cleanse, and refine their data. Whether you're a seasoned data professional or a novice user, this book is designed to elevate your proficiency in harnessing the capabilities of Power Query functions, ultimately enabling you to convert seemingly complex datasets into actionable insights.

Join me on a journey through the intricacies of Power Query functions as I demystify their functionalities, explore real-world use cases, and provide step-by-step guidance on their application. With a meticulous balance of theory and hands-on practice, *The Ultimate Guide to Functions in Power Query* is not just a book; it's your indispensable companion in mastering the art of data transformation.

Chapters include

1. "Introduction to Power Query:" Build a foundation by learning what Power Query is, its role in data transformation, and the fundamental concepts that underpin its functionality.

2. "Formatting:" Explore the nuances of formatting data, from standardizing text and numbers to customizing visual elements.

3. "Number Functions:" Discover a wealth of functions designed to manipulate and analyze numerical data, from basic arithmetic operations to advanced mathematical calculations.

4. "Text Functions:" Uncover the power of text manipulation with functions that enable you to extract, concatenate, and transform text in various ways.

5. "Date and Time Functions:" Navigate the complexities of date and time data with functions that facilitate calculations, comparisons, and conversions, ensuring accuracy in temporal analysis.

6. "List Functions:" Learn how to work with lists (ordered collections of values) using functions that allow you to manipulate, filter, and transform list-based data structures.

7. "Record Functions:" Dive into the world of records (structures that hold multiple fields of data) and harness functions to modify, extract, and manage record information.

8. "Table Functions:" Master the art of working with tables, the heart of data manipulation in Power Query, using functions that facilitate aggregation, filtering, and transformation.

9. "Extracting from Sources:" Explore how to gather data from various sources (databases, files, and folders) using functions that ensure a smooth extraction process.

10. "Other Functions:" Delve into a collection of miscellaneous functions that offer specialized capabilities, expanding your toolkit for handling unique data manipulation tasks.

Empower yourself with the expertise needed to navigate the challenges of data manipulation and unlock the true potential of your raw data. Whether you're seeking to enhance your analytical capabilities, streamline business processes, or simply gain a competitive edge, this guide is your gateway to turning data into actionable insights.

CHAPTER 1

Introduction to Power Query

In the dynamic landscape of modern data analysis, the ability to turn raw information into meaningful insights is a cornerstone of success. Welcome to the world of Power Query, an invaluable tool that empowers data professionals to tame, reshape, and amplify data, unveiling its hidden potential. This chapter serves as your gateway to understanding the essence of Power Query, its significance, and the journey you are about to embark upon.

In a data-driven era, information is abundant, sprawling across spreadsheets, databases, cloud storage, and beyond. But this information is often disparate, inconsistent, and unstructured. This is where Power Query steps in as a guiding light, enabling you to navigate through these complexities and emerge with knowledge that fuels smarter decision-making.

Your exploration begins with a foundational understanding of what Power Query truly is: a powerful data transformation tool embedded within familiar environments such as Microsoft Excel and Power BI. I'll unveil its intuitive interface, its versatile functions, and its innate ability to streamline even the most intricate data manipulation tasks.

© Omid Motamedisedeh 2024
O. Motamedisedeh, *The Ultimate Guide to Functions in Power Query*,
https://doi.org/10.1007/978-1-4842-9754-4_1

As you delve deeper, you'll grasp the essence of data transformation. Power Query empowers you to shape data to your needs, from cleaning and merging to filtering and aggregating. These transformations form the bedrock of insightful analysis, turning data from a puzzle into a clear picture.

Moreover, Power Query serves as a bridge between disparate data sources. Whether you're dealing with Excel sheets, databases, web APIs, or CSV files, Power Query offers a unified interface to access, transform, and consolidate these sources into cohesive narratives.

So, let's embark on this journey through the world of Power Query. After you navigate through the chapters to come, you'll emerge with the prowess to wield Power Query as a transformative tool, transcending data challenges and unveiling insights that lead to better, more informed decisions.

Introduction to Power Query

Power Query is a powerful tool for refining and cleaning data in Excel and Power BI. It covers the three main tasks of ETL: extract, clean, and load tables. These tasks involve

- Extracting data from various databases including SQL, Access, Microsoft Azure, and other sources like websites, Excel files, text files, and more

- Cleaning data by removing extra columns, changing value formats, adding new columns, combining tables, and so on

- Loading data (in Excel, Power Pivot, or Power BI)

This tool was introduced as an add-in for Excel 2010 and later for 2013. In these versions, by installing the add-in, a new tab called Power Query was added to Excel, as shown in Figures 1-1 and 1-2.

Figure 1-1. *Power Query tab in Excel 2010*

Figure 1-2. *Power Query tab in Excel 2013*

In Excel 2016 and later, this tool was added to the main Excel commands in the Data tab. In Excel 2021 and also 365, the commands related to Power Query are available in the Get & Transform Data group under the Data tab, and users can perform data extraction, modification, and loading processes using these commands (Figure 1-3).

Figure 1-3. *Power Query in Excel 365*

In Power BI, the commands related to Power Query are located in the Data section of the Home tab, as shown in Figure 1-4.

Figure 1-4. *Power Query in Power BI*

Power Query in Excel

In Excel, to extract values from various sources such as other Excel files, simply select the Get Data command in the Get and Transform Data section of the Data tab (Figure 1-5).

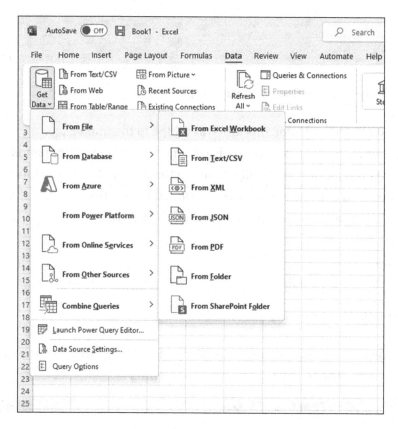

Figure 1-5. *Extracting data from an Excel file*

As you can see in Figure 1-5, different options are provided to extract the tables from different data sources. To extract values from another Excel file, select From File, and then From Excel File. The window shown in Figure 1-6 will appear and you can navigate the desired Excel file.

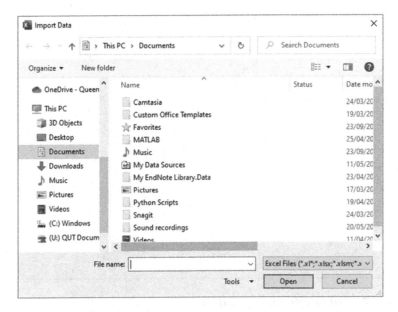

Figure 1-6. *Addressing the Excel file*

By addressing the desired Excel file (in this example, 06-Inventory. xlsx) and clicking Open, a new window will open, as shown in Figure 1-7.

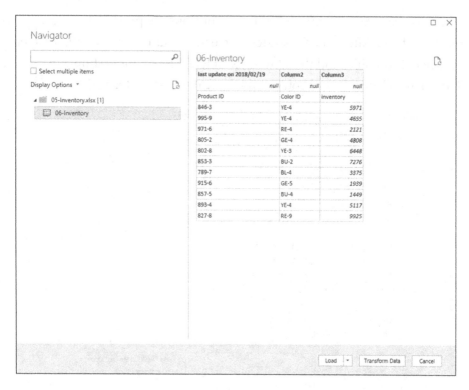

Figure 1-7. *Table selection window*

You'll see a list of all tables and sheets in the selected Excel file on the left side of this window. Depending on the user's needs, one or more tables can be selected and called in Power Query for the cleaning process. In this example, by selecting the 05-Inventory table and selecting the Transform button, the data is loaded in Power Query, as shown in Figure 1-8. (Now the data extraction process is completed.)

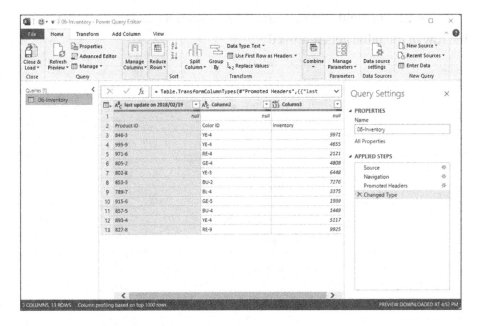

Figure 1-8. *Data extraction in Power Query*

Now you can perform the cleaning process via various commands. For example, to remove the first row of the table (empty row), simply select the Remove Top Rows command from the Reduce Rows section of the Home tab. The window shown in Figure 1-9 will appear to determine the number of rows that you want to remove from the top of the table.

Figure 1-9. *Selecting the number of rows to remove*

Enter 1 in the field and confirm it. As you can see in Figure 1-10, the first row of the table gets removed.

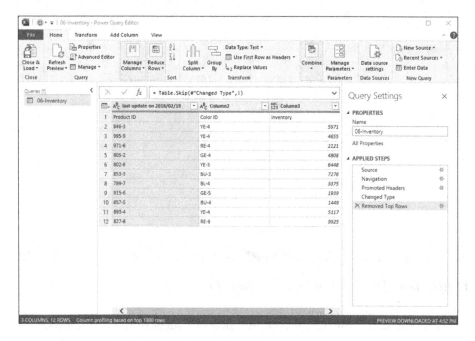

Figure 1-10. *Removing the first data row*

In the next step, to replace the column headers with the first row, select the Use first row as header command from the Transform tab. See Figure 1-11 for the result.

Figure 1-11. *Replacing column headers with the first data row*

The Product ID Column in the table shown in Figure 1-11 consists of two parts, the main part (before the dash) and a subpart (after the dash). Say you want to separate these two parts. Select the Product ID column and choose the Split By delimiter command from the Split Column section of the Home tab. See the results in Figure 1-12.

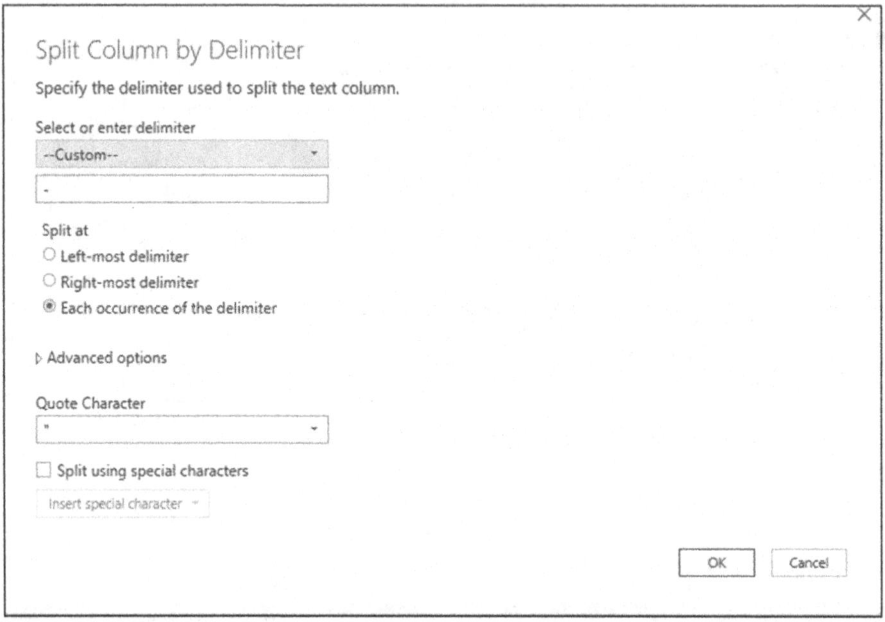

Figure 1-12. *Separating data in a column*

Then, by selecting the Custom mode according to Figure 1-12, entering a dash in the lower box, and confirming it, you'll get the result shown in Figure 1-13.

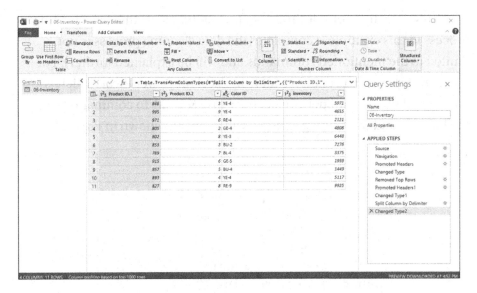

Figure 1-13. *Separated columns*

Finally, to change the names of the first and second columns to Primary ID and Secondary ID, just right-click the column headers, select Rename, and enter the desired names. See the results in Figure 1-14.

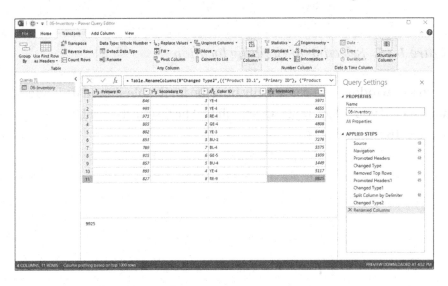

Figure 1-14. *Changing column names*

11

You've reached your desired result, so at this stage, the data cleaning process in this example is complete (the data cleaning process is not limited to the mentioned commands and will be explained further). For the final step, load the data as a table in Excel (or Power Pivot, which is considered the data model). Select the Close & Load To command from the File tab, and the loading window will appear as shown in Figure 1-15.

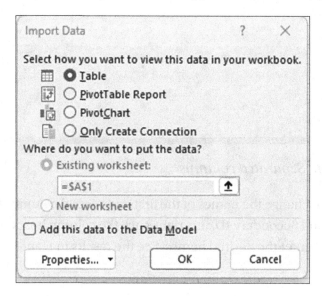

Figure 1-15. *Selecting the loading location*

In this window, you can specify how the final table should be loaded into Excel. If you select Table, the result will be visible in Excel, as seen in Figure 1-16.

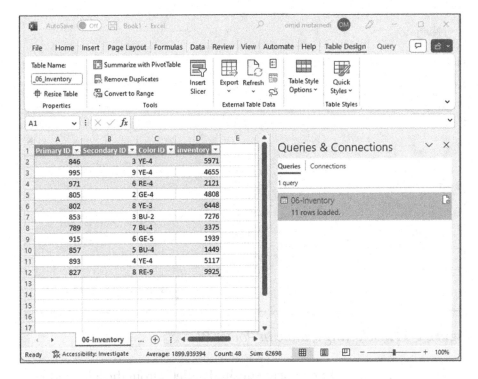

Figure 1-16. *The final table in Excel*

So, in this example, values from other Excel files were extracted, cleaned, and finally loaded as a table in the Excel file.

Power Query in Power BI

The process of using Power Query in Excel and Power BI is the same and includes the same commands. For example, to perform the process mentioned in the previous section in Power BI, just select the Excel Workbook command from the Data section of the Home tab, and then enter the address of the relevant Excel file in the opened window to see the page shown in Figure 1-17.

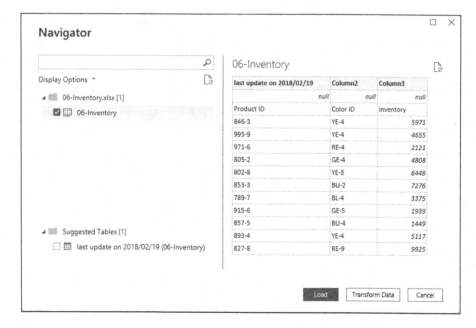

Figure 1-17. *Selecting a table in Power BI*

In this window, by selecting the desired table(s) from the left window and selecting the Transform Data command, the data will be transferred to Power Query, as you can see in Figure 1-18.

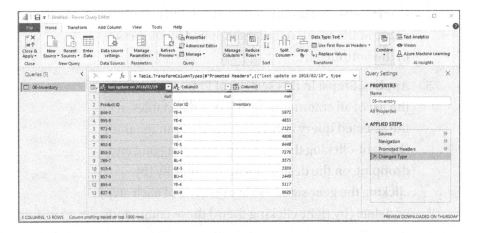

Figure 1-18. *Power Query window in Power BI*

The extraction part is finished. The data cleaning and loading processes in Power BI are like Excel, and a similar result can be obtained by performing the process explained in the previous section.

Power Query Interface

As shown in Figure 1-19, the Power Query window (in both Excel and Power BI) consists of six different parts:

1. **Queries pane**: The list of queries in the Excel or Power BI file is displayed in this section, and the user can select, modify, or group them from this section.

2. **Tabs**: The Power Query commands are displayed in this section.

3. **Formula bar**: This section is used to write a formula in Power Query, after entering the equal sign.

4. **Query setting**: This section contains the query name in the top part and the Applied Steps section in the bottom part.

5. **Applied Steps**: In this section of Power Query, the list of all commands applied to data tables in the selected query is visible. The user can rename (by right-clicking them), reorder (by dragging and dropping on the desired location), modify (by clicking the gear sign beside the name of each step) or delete (by right-clicking them) these commands.

6. **Preview pane**: In this section, the result of the selected command from the Applied Steps section is displayed.

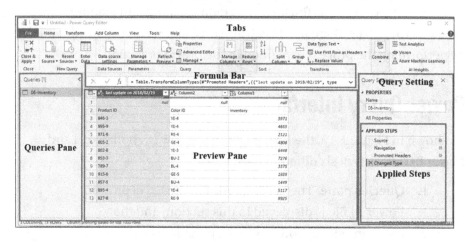

Figure 1-19. *Different parts of the Power Query window*

M Code

To reopen the Power Query window and modify the created query in the Excel file, the Queries & Connections mode from the Data section of the Home tab in the Excel should be activated. A list of active queries will be shown in the Queries and Connections section (Figure 1-20). The queries can be modified by right-clicking them and selecting the Edit option.

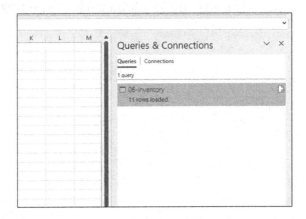

Figure 1-20. *Queries & Connections command*

The result of query will be shown, as you can see in Figure 1-21.

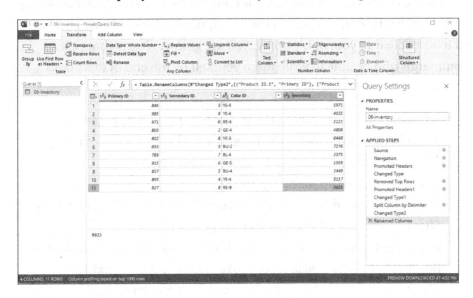

Figure 1-21. *Changing column names*

The query can be modified step by step in the Applied Step section or can be modified altogether by selecting the Advanced Editor command in the Home tab, which will lead to the result shown in Figure 1-22.

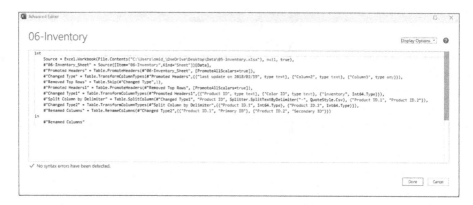

Figure 1-22. *Advance Editor*

The Advanced Editor window contains all the steps taken in extracting and cleaning the data, written in the M language, which is shown below. (If it is not clear to you, don't worry. You are going to learn about these commands and be able to write them yourself by the end of this book)

```
Let
    Source = Excel.Workbook(File.Contents("C:\Users\omid_\
    OneDrive\Desktop\Data\05-Inventory.xlsx"), null, true),
    #"06-Inventory_Sheet" = Source{[Item="06-
    Inventory",Kind="Sheet"]}[Data],
    #"Promoted Headers" = Table.PromoteHeaders(#"06-Inventory_
    Sheet", [PromoteAllScalars=true]),
    #"Changed Type" = Table.TransformColumnTypes(#"Promoted
    Headers",{{"last update on 2018/02/19", type text},
    {"Column2", type text}, {"Column3", type any}}),
    #"Removed Top Rows" = Table.Skip(#"Changed Type",1),
```

```
#"Promoted Headers1" = Table.PromoteHeaders(#"Removed Top
Rows", [PromoteAllScalars=true]),
#"Changed Type1" = Table.TransformColumnTypes(#"Promoted
Headers1",{{"Product ID", type text}, {"Color ID", type
text}, {"inventory", Int64.Type}}),
#"Split Column by Delimiter" = Table.SplitColumn(#"Changed
Type1", "Product ID", Splitter.SplitTextByDelimiter("-",
QuoteStyle.Csv), {"Product ID.1", "Product ID.2"}),
#"Changed Type2" = Table.TransformColumnTypes(#"Split
Column by Delimiter",{{"Product ID.1", Int64.Type},
{"Product ID.2", Int64.Type}}),
#"Renamed Columns" = Table.RenameColumns(#"Changed
Type2",{{"Product ID.1", "Primary ID"}, {"Product ID.2",
"Secondary ID"}})
in
    #"Renamed Columns"
```

By performing each of the commands in the cleaning process (e.g., renaming columns, splitting the Product ID column, or removing the first row), a line is added to the previous commands. Each command line consists of two parts separated by an equal sign. The variable name (which is also shown in the Applied Steps section) is on the left side of the equal sign, and the calculation formula for that variable is on the right side. For example, in the following command, the variable name is #"Removed Top Rows" and the Table.Skip function is used to calculate it as follows:

```
#"Removed Top Rows" = Table.Skip(#"Changed Type",1)
```

In this example, the Table.Skip function receives the table with the name #"Changed Type" (which was calculated in the previous step) and removes the first row. Then it displays the new table as output. Therefore, the value of the variable #"Removed Top Rows" is equal to a table.

Generally, Table.Skip is defined in Power Query as follows:

```
Table.Skip(
    table as table,
    optional countOrCondition as any
    ) as table
```

This function has two inputs (separated by a comma). The first input is a table as table, which means that the first input is in the table format which is called Table (the input type is specified after the as), and the second input is optional (because of the use of the word Optional) and is named countOrCondition with a format of any. Finally, since the table expression is registered at the end of the function, the output of this function is always a table.

In another line of this code, the variable #"Changed Type2" is defined as follows:

```
#"Changed Type2" = Table.TransformColumnTypes(#"Split Column
by Delimiter",{{"Product ID.1", Int64.Type}, {"Product ID.2",
Int64.Type}})
```

To increase the readability of this command, it can be displayed in several lines as follows:

```
#"Changed Type2" = Table.TransformColumnTypes(
#"Split Column by Delimiter",
{{"Product ID.1", Int64.Type}, {"Product ID.2", Int64.Type}}
)
```

As you can see in this command, the Table.TransformColumnTypes function uses two different arguments; the first is in the type of table, and the second variable is in the type of list.

Conclusion

In this chapter, you were introduced to Power Query, an essential tool for data transformation and manipulation in various data analysis and visualization contexts. This is the beginning of your Power Query journey. In this chapter, a simple example of a Power Query application was provided so you could get familiar with the basic features of Power Query and the M language. You also learned the role of the M language in data transformations. You also saw the use of commands to clean the values in a table. In the rest of this book, all of the main functions will be explained in depth.

The next chapter delves deeper into the types of data in Power Query including, null, logical values, number, text, list, records, and binary.

CHAPTER 2

Data Types

Like any other software, Power Query supports different data types (formats) and provides a wide range of functions for modifying values based on their types. Power Query supports simple data types such as numbers, text, and time/date as well as complex data types like lists, tables, and binary. This chapter focuses on understanding the fundamental data types used in Power Query and their characteristics plus handling type conversions. By the end of this chapter, you will have a solid understanding of how to effectively manage and manipulate different data types within Power Query, setting the stage for more advanced data transformation and analysis in subsequent chapters.

Data Types in Power Query

Since each function in Power Query can be applied on the values with a specific data format, the value's type is very important in this software. To describe the importance of data types, consider a simple function like Text.Start. It is used to extract the first characters of a text. If the first input is text, the output of this function will be equal to some of the initial characters of that text, but if the first input is not in the text format, the output will be an error. Therefore, based on the type of input, the result of this function will be different and may lead to an error, as shown in Table 2-1.

© Omid Motamedisedeh 2024
O. Motamedisedeh, *The Ultimate Guide to Functions in Power Query*,
https://doi.org/10.1007/978-1-4842-9754-4_2

Table 2-1. *Samples of Text.Start*

Formula	Result
=Text.Start("Hello",3)	"Hel"
=Text.Start("1232",2)	"12"
=Text.Start(1232,2)	Error

Therefore, knowing the format of your data and how to convert different data formats into others is very important. Table 2-2 shows the types of data along with their definitions in Power Query.

Table 2-2. *Power Query Data Types*

Definition	Data type
Null	*Null*
true/false	*Logical*
0 1 -1 1.5 2.3e-5	*Number*
#time(09,15,00)	*Time*
#date(2013,02,26)	*Date*
#datetime(2013,02,26, 09,15,00)	*DateTime*
#datetimezone(2013,02,26, 09,15,00, 09,00)	*DateTimeZone*
#duration(0,1,30,0)	*Duration*
"hello"	*Text*
#binary("AQID")	*Binary*
{1, 2, 3}	*List*
[A = 1, B = 2]	*Record*
#table({"X","Y"},{{0,1},{1,0}})	*Table*
(x) => x + 1	*Function*
type { number } type table [A = any, B = text]	*Type*

Null

The value of null is used instead of missing values in Power Query and is defined as null. Some mathematical operations can be done on the null values. Assuming that the variable x is equal to null and y is a none null value, various mathematical operations and their results are shown in Table 2-3.

Table 2-3. *Operations on Null Values*

Formula	Result
x > y	null
x >= y	null
x < y	null
x <= y	null
x = y	null
x <> y	null
x ?? y	y
y ?? x	y

Logical Values

The logical value type of data, with the symbol of , includes two states: true or false. To compare the values in this group, true can be considered equivalent to the number 1 and false can be considered equivalent to the number 0.

Generally, logical values are obtained by comparing one value with another (for example, 2>3) or the output of information functions such as Number.IsOdd.

If x and y are equal to logical values, the use of mathematical operators as well as logical operators (including and, or, and not) as x and y, x or y, and not x are the main operations on these values.

Numbers

The numbers type includes a large range of numerical values (integer and decimal). In addition to numbers, there are two values named #infinity (obtained from dividing a positive number by zero) and #-infinity (obtained from dividing a negative number by zero) that represent positive infinity (the largest possible number) and negative infinity (the smallest possible number) and they are also included in this group of data.

The #nan value, equal to dividing zero by zero, is also included in this group of data type. Generally, any mathematical and comparison operations such as x > y, x >= y, x < y, x <= y, x = y, x <> y, x + y, x - y, x * y, x / y, x ?? y, and +x can be performed on numbers x and y in Power Query.

Different number formats are provided in Table 2-4.

Table 2-4. Number Formats

Description	Symbol	Data Format
This data format represents decimal numbers and is one of the most used formats for numbers. This format can include all negative decimal numbers within the range of -1.79E+308 to -2.23E-308, as well as all positive decimal numbers within the range of 2.23E-308 to 1.79E+308, including the number 0.	1.2	**Decimal number**
This format, known as Currency in Excel, has a specific decimal place and can display numbers with four decimal places and 19 digits before the decimal point.	$	**Fixed decimal number**
This format is used to display integer numbers, and the decimal part is not displayed. This format can display all numbers in the range of -9,223,372,036,854,775,807 (-2^63+1) to 9,223,372,036,854,775,806 (2^63-2).	$1^2{}_3$	**Whole number**
This format is very like the format used to display decimal numbers, except that numbers are displayed with percentage symbol.	%	**Percentage**

Time and Date

There are different formats of data for displaying information as time and date in Power Query. Times in Power Query are defined as #time(Hour, Minute, Second), where the first input must be between 0 and 23, and the second and third inputs must be between 0 and 59.

Along with time, dates in Power Query are defined as #date(Year, Month, Day), where the input value for Year is between 1 and 9999, and the other two parameters accept numbers between 1 and 12 and 1 and 31, respectively.

To enter the value of date and time simultaneously, #datetime(year, month, day, hour, minute, second) can be used. In a more comprehensive form of this type of data, datetimezone can be used as shown here:

```
#datetimezone(
        year, month, day,
        hour, minute, second,
        offset-hours, offset-minutes)
```

in which the allowed range for each input is as follows:

$$1 \leq \text{year} \leq 9999$$

$$1 \leq \text{month} \leq 12$$

$$1 \leq \text{day} \leq 31$$

$$0 \leq \text{hour} \leq 23$$

$$0 \leq \text{minute} \leq 59$$

$$0 \leq \text{second} \leq 59$$

$$-14 \leq \text{offset-hours} \leq 14$$

$$-59 \leq \text{offset-minutes} \leq 59$$

Another type of data in this group represents a duration, which is equal to the difference between two time or date values. This data type is defined as #duration(day, hour, minute, second) in Power Query. Generally, in addition to the date and time functions, any mathematical calculations or comparison operations can be performed on this type of data.

The features of date-related formats are covered in Table 2-5.

Table 2-5. *Date Formats*

Description	Symbol	Data Format
This format is used to display dates, and it can display any date in the range of year 1900 to 9999.		**Date**
Each date value can be determined by an integer number where the date January 1, 1900 is considered equivalent to 1; January 2, 1900 is equal to 2; and so on. So, by converting the number 365 to the date value, the equivalent date will be provided as January 1, 1901.		
This format is used to express time. Time is equivalent to a positive decimal number less than 1. Therefore, by considering 24 hours equivalent to the number 1, 12 noon is equivalent to 0.5 and 6 am is equivalent to 0.25.		**Time**
This format is used for values to show the date and time beside each other. Each Date/Time value is equivalent to a decimal number where the date part is determined by an integer and the time part is determined by decimal number.		**Date/Time**
This format is like the date and time format. The difference is that the time zone is also considered during calculations. However, after loading the data into the data model and considering the effective value of the time zone, the result is presented as a simple date and time format.		**Date/Time /Timezone**
This format represents the time interval between two dates or times.		**Duration**

Text

The text format, with the symbol of $^A{}_C^B$, includes a wide range of values and must be enclosed in double quotes (" ") to define them, such as "ABC" or even "2." The text format is used in Power Query for text with a length of up to 268 million characters. When a number is entered inside double quotes, its format is converted to text and mathematical operations are no longer performed on it. Among the types of operators, comparison operators (<=>), the operator for checking null values, and & operator for concatenating two texts can be used for text values.

Binary

In Power Query, a binary value, with the symbol of ▤, is equal to a string of bits contained in files with a special format. For example, to call information from an Excel file as tables within Power Query, first the information is called up as binary values and then it is converted to tables using various functions.

List

Lists include a set of values (with different data types) in a specific order. For simplicity, a list can be considered as a column in a table without a title. In Power Query, to define a list, simply place the desired values inside { } and separate them from each other using commas. For example, different examples of lists are given here:

=\{1,2,3,4\}

=\{1,2,3,\{4,5\}\}

=\{1,"a",2,"B",\{"C","D"\}\}

=\{[a=1,b=2],2,\{1\},\{1,2\},[c=2],[d=\{1,2,3,\}]\}

Record

Another type of data in Power Query is the record. For simplicity, records can be considered as a single row of a table, where each value has a header (or title) and there is just a value for each title. To define a record, it is sufficient to enter the field title and its value inside [ ], separating different fields with a comma, such as [a=1,b=2]

In the previous example, the record has two fields with the names a and b, and their values are 1 and 2, respectively. There are no limitations in the type of values in a record, and they can include various types such as lists, records, and tables. Here are different examples of records:

[a=1,v={1,2,3,4}]

[a=[b=1,c=2],d=[e={1,2,3,4},f=null]]

[a="xyz",b={1,2,3}]

Table

A table is a data format in which values are organized in rows with specific column titles. The data in a table can have various formats, and there are different functions in Power Query to manage tables. Tables can be created directly in Power Query or called from other sources.

Function

Another type of data is a function, which will be explained in detail in future chapters.

Type Conversion

There are several functions in Power Query for converting different data formats into another, but before getting familiar with them, it should be noted that not every data format can be converted to another format. For example, you cannot convert the text format "Hello" to a number with any function.

The possibility of converting between different data formats in Power Query is shown in Figure 2-1.

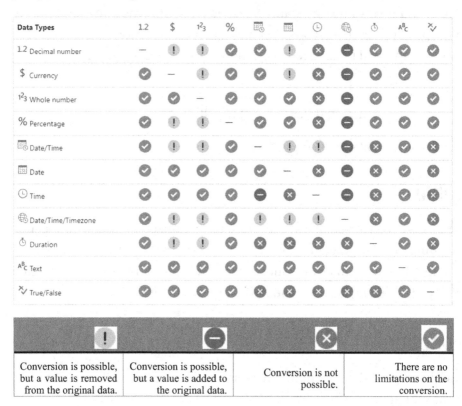

Figure 2-1. *Data conversion in Power Query*

There are multiple functions in Power Query to convert different data formats to each other, and the most important ones are provided in the rest of this chapter.

Converting Values to the Number Format

The functions related to converting values with different formats to the number format are listed in Table 2-6. All of these functions receive an input of a specific type, and their output is a value in the format of number.

Table 2-6. Converting Values to the Number Format

Function	Description
Number.FromText(text as text) as number	Using this function, numerical values that are stored in text format can be converted to numbers. For example, if the number 123 is stored as text, this function can be used to convert it to a number.
Number.From(value as any) as number	This function is used to convert a numerical value stored in other formats to a number format.
Int32.From(value as any) as number	This function is used to convert a value to a 32-bit integer representation.
Int64.From(value as any) as number	This function is used to convert a value to a 64-bit integer representation.
Single.From(value as any) as number	This function returns a single number value from the given value.
Double.From(value as any) as number	This function returns a double number value from the given value.
Decimal.From(value as any) as number	This function returns a decimal number from the given value.
Currency.From(value as any) as number	This function returns a currency value from the given value.

Converting Values to the Text Format

The list of functions for converting values with a different format to the text format is provided in Table 2-7. All of these functions receive an input of a specific type, and their output is in the format of text.

Table 2-7. *Converting Values to the Text Format*

Function	Description
Text.From(value as any) as text	This function is used to convert a value in any format to text.
Number.ToText(number as number) as text	This function is used to convert a value in the number format to a value in the format of text.
Logical.ToText(logical as logical) as text	Using this function, the value True/False is converted to text.
Date.ToText(date as date) as text	Using this function, a date format value can be converted to a text format value.
Time.ToText (time as time) as text	Using this function, a time format value can be converted to a text format value.
DateTime.ToText (datetime as datetime) as text	Using this function, date and time format values can be converted to a text format value.
DateTimeZone.ToText (datetimezone as datetimezone) as text	Using this function, a date, time, and timezone format value can be converted to a text format value.

Converting Values to the Date and Time Format

There are several functions for converting values with different formats to date, which are listed in Table 2-8.

Table 2-8. *Converting Values to the Date Format*

Function	Description
Date.FromText(text as text) as date	This function is used to convert a text value to a date.
Time.FromText (text as text) as time	This function is used to convert a text value to time.
DateTime.FromText (text as text) as datetime	This function is used to convert a text value to a date and time.
DateTimeZone.FromText (text as text) as datetimezone	This function is used to convert a text value to a date, time, and timezone.
Date.From(value as any) as date	This function is used to convert a value with any format to date.
Time.From (value as any) as time	This function is used to convert a value with any format to a time.
DateTime.From (value as any) as datetime	This function is used to convert a value with any format to a date and time.
DateTimeZone.From (value as any) as datetimezone	This function is used to convert a value with any format to a date, time, and timezone.

Converting Values to the Record Format

There are several functions for converting values in the date and time format to a value in the record format; see Table 2-9.

Table 2-9. *Converting Date Values to the Record Format*

Function	Description
Date.ToRecord(date as date) as record	Using this function, a date format value can be converted to a text format value.
Time.ToRecord(time as time) as record	Using this function, a time format value can be converted to a text format value.
DateTime.ToRecord (datetime as datetime) as record	Using this function, a date and time format value can be converted to a text format value.
DateTimeZone.ToRecord (datetimezone as datetimezone) as record	Using this function, a date, time, and timezone format value can be converted to a text format value.

Conclusion

In this chapter, you explored different data types in Power Query and their features. You learned about the possibility of changing data types and the functions for data types conversions. You also learned about errors that might happen from by using the wrong data types.

Now that you have mastered data types, you are ready to learn about functions for manipulating values with different data types. In the next chapter, the functions for working on values with the number type are presented.

CHAPTER 3

Number Functions

This chapter delves into the realm of numeric data manipulation and analysis within Power Query. These functions allow you to perform various mathematical calculations and transformations on numeric data. These functions are essential for manipulating numerical values within your data, performing calculations, and generating insights. Number functions can be applied to individual numeric values and columns of numeric data, or they can be used in combination with other functions to create complex calculations. The functions in this chapter are categorized into six groups, which will be discussed in the rest of this chapter.

Constant Values

In Power Query, there are several functions that generate constant values and they are mentioned in Table 3-1. These functions do not need any argument, and they are used with opening and closing parenthesis.

© Omid Motamedisedeh 2024
O. Motamedisedeh, *The Ultimate Guide to Functions in Power Query*,
https://doi.org/10.1007/978-1-4842-9754-4_3

Table 3-1. *Functions for Constant Values*

Formula	Description
Number.E	The value of this formula is always equal to the number e (2.718...).
Number.Epsilon	The result of this function is equal to the smallest number in the power query, which is equal to 4.9 e-394.
Number.NaN	This function is equal to the result of dividing zero by zero.
Number.NegativeInfinity	The output of this function is negative infinity, which is equal to dividing any negative number by zero.
Number.PI	The result of this function is the π number (3.14...).
Number.PositiveInfinity	The result of this function is positive infinity, which is equal to dividing any positive number by zero.

Information Functions

In Power Query, there are three functions to check if a value odd, even, or NaN and they are listed in Table 3-2. All of these functions receive a numerical input and based on its value, the result of the function will be True or False.

Table 3-2. *Functions for Number Information*

Function	Description
Number.IsEven	The result will be True if its input is an even number.
Number.IsNaN	The result will be True if its input argument is NaN.
Number.IsOdd	The result will be True if its input is an odd number.

Table 3-3 shows applications of these functions.

Table 3-3. *Application of Number Information Functions*

Function	Result
Number.IsEven(2)	True
Number.IsEven(3)	False
Number.IsNaN(2)	False
Number.IsNaN(2/0)	False
Number.IsNaN(0/0)	True
Number.IsOdd(2)	False
Number.IsOdd(3)	True

Rounding Operation

For rounding numbers in Power Query, the functions listed in Table 3-4 can be used. All of these functions receive two arguments:

1. The number (that you want to round) is entered in the first argument.

2. The rounding precision is determined in the second argument. Entering 2 in this input means rounding the number up to 2 decimal places and entering 0 means rounding the numbers after the decimal. To round two digits before the decimal, -2 can be entered in this input.

Table 3-4. *Number Rounding Functions*

Function	Description
Number.RoundDown	This function performs the rounding operation towards a smaller number. (The output of this function is always smaller than the inputted number in the first argument.)
Number.RoundUp	This function performs the rounding operation towards a larger number. (The output of this function is always larger than the inputted number in the first argument.)
Number.RoundAwayFromZero	If the input is a positive number, its calculation logic is consistent with Number.RoundUp, and if its input is a negative number, its calculation logic is like Number.RoundDown.
Number.RoundTowardZero	If the input is a positive number, its calculation logic is consistent with Number.RoundDown, and if its input is a negative number, its calculation logic is like Number.RoundUp.

In addition to the functions mentioned in Table 3-4, there is another function in Power Query called Number.Round with three arguments. The first two arguments are in accordance with the inputs of other rounding functions, and the third input, which is optional, determines the logic of the calculation and can be one of cases shown in Table 3-5.

Table 3-5. *The Third Input of Number.Round*

Parameters	Value	Description
RoundingMode.Up	0	In this case, the function works according to the logic of Number. RoundUp.
RoundingMode.Down	1	In this case, it works according to the logic of Number.RoundDown.
RoundingMode.AwayFromZero	2	In this case, it works according to the logic of Number. RoundAwayFromZero.
RoundingMode.TowardZero	3	In this case, it works according to the logic of Number. RoundTowardZero.
RoundingMode.ToEven	4	In this case, the corresponding number is rounded to the nearest even number.

The default calculation mode of this function is RoundingMode.ToEven, so the result of the following formulas is 4:

$$= \text{Number.Round}(4.5)$$

$$= \text{Number.Round}(3.5)$$

The results of rounding functions for different examples are provided in Table 3-6.

Table 3-6. *Application of Number Rounding Functions*

	Number.Round	Number.RoundUp	Number.RoundDown	Number.RoundAwayFromZero	Number.RoundTowardZero
(162.9183,3)	162.918	162.919	162.918	162.919	162.918
(162.9183,2)	162.92	162.92	162.91	162.92	162.91
(162.9183,0)	163	163	162	163	162
(162.9183,-1)	160	170	160	170	160
(162.9183,-2)	200	200	100	200	100
(-162.9183,3)	-162.918	-162.918	-162.919	-162.919	-162.918
(-162.9183,2)	-162.92	-162.91	-162.92	-162.92	-162.91
(-162.9183,0)	-163	-162	-163	-163	-162
(-162.9183,-1)	-160	-160	-170	-170	-160

Mathematical Operations

In performing mathematical operations on numbers in Power Query, there are two groups of functions. Functions in the first group, listed in Table 3-7, receive a numerical value and perform mathematical calculations on it based on the function's type.

Table 3-7. *Mathematical Operation Functions*

Function	Description
Number.Abs	The output is equal to the absolute value of the input number.
Number.Sign	If the input number is positive, the result will be 1. If the input value is negative, the result will be -1. If the input is 0, the result of this function will be zero.
Number.Sqrt	The result is equal to the square root of the inputted number.
Number.Exp	The result is equal to the e number raised to the power of the input number.
Number.Factorial	The result is equal to the factorial of the inputted number.
Number.Log10	The result is equal to the logarithm of the input number in base 10.
Number.Ln	The result is equal to the logarithm of input in the base of e.

The functions in the second group receive two inputs, a and b, and result as in Table 3-8 based on the used function.

Table 3-8. *Number Mathematical Functions*

Function	Description
Number.IntegerDivide	The result is equal to the integer part of the division of number a by b.
Number.Log	The result is equal to the logarithm of number a in base b.
Number.Mod	The result is equal to the remainder of the division of number a by b.
Number.Power	The result is equal to number a raised to the power of number b

Several examples of these functions are provided in Table 3-9.

Table 3-9. *Sample Mathematical Functions*

Function	Result	Function	Result
Number.Abs(12.5)	12.5	Number.Abs(-12.5)	-12.5
Number.Sign(12.5)	1	Number.Sign(-12.5)	-1
Number.Sqrt(4)	2	Number.Sqrt(9)	3
Number.Exp(1)	2.7182	Number.Exp(2)	7.389
Number.Factorial(3)	6	Number.Factorial(4)	24
Number.Log10(10)	1	Number.Log10(100)	2
Number.Ln(1)	0	Number.Ln(2)	0.693
Number.IntegerDivide(40,3)	13	Number.IntegerDivide(5,2)	2
Number.Log(25,5)	2	Number.Log(9,3)	2
Number.Mod(40,3)	1	Number.Mod(5,2)	1
Number.Power(2,3)	8	Number.Power(2,4)	16

Random Generation

Number.Random and Number.RandomBetween are used in Power Query to generate random numbers. Number.Random does not take any argument and is defined as Number.Random(), always resulting in a random number between 0 and 1. The function Number.RandomBetween takes two numbers a and b and always outputs a decimal random number between a and b.

Trigonometry

Trigonometric functions in Power Query, like other software, include three groups of basic, hyperbolic, and inverse trigonometric functions, listed in Table 3-10.

Table 3-10. *Trigonometry Functions*

Inverse	Hyperbolic	Basic
Number.Asin	Number.Sinh	Number.Sin
Number.Acos	Number.Cosh	Number.Cos
Number.Atan	Number.Tanh	Number.Tan
Number.Atan2		

Conclusion

This chapter introduced you to the functions that manipulate numbers in Power Query. These functions are categorized into the following six groups.

- Constant values include all functions that result in a general number, like the Pi number.

- Information functions include functions used to determine the type of numbers, such as checking whether a number is odd or even.

- Rounding number functions include functions that are used for rounding operations.

- Mathematical operation functions are used for exponential, logarithmic, trigonometric calculations, and such.

- Random generation functions include functions that are used to ensure accurate calculations and results through proper rounding strategies.

- Trigonometry functions like `Number.Sin`, `Number.Cos`, and `Number.Tan` are used for trigonometry calculations.

To complete your journey of learning the functions for operating on basic data types, you'll explore the functions for manipulating text values, such as combining texts or extracting a specific part of a text, in the next chapter.

CHAPTER 4

Text Functions

In the realm of data transformation and manipulation, text data stands as a foundational building block. Whether dealing with customer names, product descriptions, log entries, or any other textual content, the ability to extract, cleanse, and transform text becomes paramount. This is where the prowess of Power Query truly shines. In this chapter, you will delve into the art of harnessing text functions within Power Query, unveiling a toolkit that empowers data professionals to conquer the complexities of unstructured and semi-structured text data.

Your journey through this chapter will commence with the fundamentals such as understanding the nuances of text encoding, manipulation, and the role of Power Query's text functions in these processes. You'll explore how to efficiently extract specific elements from strings, like isolating URLs from paragraphs or capturing dates from lengthy narratives.

As you traverse deeper, you'll uncover the potential of text functions to cleanse and standardize data. From removing extraneous spaces and punctuation to converting case formats, these operations are the bedrock of consistent and reliable text analysis.

These functions are categorized into the following five groups:

- Extracting part of a text
- Removing, replacing, and combining texts
- Text corrections

O. Motamedisedeh, *The Ultimate Guide to Functions in Power Query*, https://doi.org/10.1007/978-1-4842-9754-4_4

- Searching for characters in the reference texts

- Text conversion

Extracting Part of a Text

In this part of text-related functions in Power Query, those related to extracting the characters from a text are explained. These functions are used to extract the values based on their position from the beginning, middle, or end of the texts.

Text.At

Text.At is used to extract a character (only one character) within a text based on its position, as follows:

```
Text.At(
        text as nullable text,
        index as number
        ) as nullable text
```

This function receives the following two arguments, and its result is always a character within a reference text:

1. The reference text is entered in the first argument.

2. The second input (as a number) determines the position of character that you want to extract from the reference text. (Numbering starts from 0.)

Table 4-1 shows the different uses of this function.

Table 4-1. *Examples of Text.At*

Formula	Result
= Text.At("XNW-11-1",0)	"X"
= Text.At("XNW-11-1",1)	"N"
= Text.At("XNW-11-1",3)	"-"

Text.Start

Text.Start is used to extract a specific number of characters from the beginning of a text, as follows:

```
Text.Start(
    text as nullable text,
    count as number
) as nullable text
```

This function has the following two arguments:

1. The reference text. (The first input of this function must be in text format; otherwise, the result of the function is equal to an error.)

2. The number of characters to be extracted from the beginning of the text is defined as the second input of this function.

Entering the number 2 in the second input result in the first two characters of the reference text. To further examine this function, multiple examples are provided in Table 4-2.

Table 4-2. *Examples of Text.Start*

Formula	Result
=Text.Start("Xn1281",2)	"Xn"
=Text.Start("Xn1281",3)	"Xn1"
=Text.Start("Xn1281",1)	"X"
=Text.Start(121,2)	Error

The result of the last formula is Error, because the first input is entered as a number but a text value should be entered. So, in this case before using Text.Start, you need to convert the first input to text by another function like Text.From. Therefore, the corrected version of the last formula is as follows:

=Text.Start(Text.From(121),2)

In this case, the result of the function is equal to "12".

Text.End

The definition of this function is like Text.Start, but this function is used to extract a specific number of characters from the end of the reference text.

```
Text.End(
    text as nullable text,
    count as number
) as nullable text
```

This function has the following two inputs:

1. The first input specifies the reference text whose end characters you want to extract.

2. The number of characters for extraction is determined in the second input.

Table 4-3 shows several applications of this function.

Table 4-3. *Examples of Text.End*

Formula	Result
=Text.End("Xn1281",2)	"81"
=Text.End("Xn1281",3)	"281"
=Text.End("Xn1281",1)	"1"

The output of this function is always a text and is not summable unless you convert the result to a number before using it in the formula.

Text.Range

Another function for extracting characters in a text is Text.Range. It is used for extracting the middle characters of a text as follows:

```
Text.Range(
        text as nullable text,
        offset as number,
        optional count as nullable number
        ) as nullable text
```

This function takes three arguments:

1. The first argument defines the reference text.

2. The second argument determines the starting point of the extraction (from which character you want to extract the characters).

3. The number of characters to be extracted is specified in the third argument.

In this function, entering the value "Xn192" in the first input, the number 2 in the second input, and the number 1 in the third input means that separation starts from the third character (characters' positions start from 0) and only one character should be extracted. Therefore, the result is "1".

Table 4-4 shows different examples of this function.

Table 4-4. *Examples of Text.Range*

Formula	Result
=Text.Range("Xn1281",2,1)	"1"
=Text.Range("Xn1281",0,3)	"Xn1"
=Text.Range("Xn1281",1,2)	"n1"
=Text.Range("Xn1281",3,12)	Error

Based on the last example in Table 4-4, the result of Text. Range("Xn1281",3,12) is an error. In this formula, you are searching for 12 characters after the third character in the referenced text, but there are only three characters of "381" after the third character, so the result of this function is an error. In this case, Text.Middle can be used. The argument of this function is the same as Text.Range but the difference is that the result of Text.Middle("Xn1281",3,12) is equal to "281".

In Text.Middle, the third argument is optional. If you don't enter a value for this argument, the separation continues to the end of the reference text.

Text.AfterDelimiter

Text.AfterDelimiter is used to extract a part of a text after a specific delimiter, as follows:

```
Text.AfterDelimiter(
        text as nullable text,
```

```
delimiter as text,
optional index as any
        ) as any
```

This function takes three arguments:

1. The first argument is the reference text.

2. The delimiter for determining the starting point for separation is entered in the second argument. It is entered as a text value.

3. If the delimiter has been repeated several times within the reference text, the third input is used to specify which repetition should be considered for separation (counting starts from 0). This input is optional, and if not entered, the number 0 is considered instead.

The output of this function is always a part of the reference text that comes after the delimiter. To clarify this function, various examples are provided in Table 4-5.

Table 4-5. *Examples of Text.AfterDelimiter*

Formula	Result
`= Text.AfterDelimiter("XNW-11-181-M","-")`	"11-181-M"
`= Text.AfterDelimiter("XNW-11-181-M","-",0)`	"11-181-M"
`= Text.AfterDelimiter("XNW-11-181-M","-",1)`	"181-M"
`= Text.AfterDelimiter("XNW-11-181-M","-",2)`	"M"
`= Text.AfterDelimiter("FMn12N16","N")`	"16"
`= Text.AfterDelimiter("FMn12N16","n")`	"12N16"
`= Text.AfterDelimiter("XNW-11-181-M","u",2)`	

For the last example in Table 4-5, the result will be empty if the reference text is not included the delimiter.

In the third input, beside entering a number to determine the desired repetition of the delimiter in the reference text, the searching direction for the delimiter in the reference text can be specified by entering RelativePosition. FromStart or RelativePosition.FromEnd beside the number in a list.

For example, the following formula results in the characters after the first "-" and is equal to "11-181-M":

```
= Text.AfterDelimiter(
"XNW-11-181-M",
"-",
0)
```

In another example, the result of the following formula is the same, but it is emphasized that it is searching for the first "-" from the beginning of the text (left to right):

```
= Text.AfterDelimiter(
"XNW-11-181-M",
"-",
{0,RelativePosition.FromStart})
```

But by using the following formula, the result is different. In this case, you are looking for the text after the first dash, but it is emphasized to search for the first "-" from the end of the text (right to left). So, the result of the function is equal to "M":

```
= Text.AfterDelimiter(
"XNW-11-181-M",
"-",
{0,RelativePosition.FromEnd})
```

Text.BeforeDelimiter

Text.BeforeDelimiter is defined like Text.AfterDelimiter and is used to extract the characters before the delimiter in the reference text. This function is defined in Power Query as follows:

```
Text.BeforeDelimiter(
        text as nullable text,
        delimiter as text,
        optional index as any
                    ) as any
```

This function takes three arguments as follows:

1. The reference text is entered in the first argument.

2. In the second input, the delimiter is entered as a text value.

3. If the delimiter is repeated several times within the text, the third input is used to specify which occurrence should be considered for separation. This input is optional, and if not entered, the number 0 is considered instead.

The output of this function is always a part of the reference text before the delimiter (defined in the second input). To clarify this function, various examples are provided in Table 4-6.

Table 4-6. *Examples of Text.BeforeDelimiter*

Formula	Result
= Text.BeforeDelimiter ("XNW-11-181-M","-")	"XNW"
= Text.BeforeDelimiter("XNW-11-181-M","-",0)	"XNW"
= Text.BeforeDelimiter("XNW-11-181-M","-",1)	"XNW-11"
= Text.BeforeDelimiter("XNW-11-181-M","-",2)	"XNW-11-181"

As with Text.AfterDelimiter, by using RelativePosition.FromStart or RelativePosition.FromEnd plus the entered number in the third input as a form of list, the direction for searching the desired occurrence of the delimiter in the reference text can be changed.

For example, the following formula indicates that the text registered before the first "-" should be displayed as output. The result of the function is "XNW".

```
= Text.BeforeDelimiter("XNW-11-181-M","-",0)
```

The result of the following formula is the same as the above formula, except that this formula displays the text before the first "-" by searching from the beginning of the reference text (left side):

```
= Text.BeforeDelimiter(

"XNW-11-181-M",

"-",

{0,RelativePosition.FromStart})
```

The next formula extracts the text before the first dash by searching from end of the reference text (close to the end of the text). Therefore, the result of the function is "XNW-11-181".

```
= Text.BeforeDelimiter(

"XNW-11-181-M",

"-",

{0,RelativePosition.FromEnd})
```

Text.BetweenDelimiters

Text.BetweenDelimiters is used to separate a part of text between two delimiters, such as between "-" and "/" as follows:

```
Text.BetweenDelimiters(
        text as nullable text,
        startDelimiter as text,
        endDelimiter as text,
        optional startIndex as any,
        optional endIndex as any
                    ) as any
```

This function takes the following five arguments:

1. The first input of this function represents the reference text.

2. The second input determines the delimiter for determining the separation starting point.

3. The desired delimiter for determining the ending point of the separation is specified in the third input of this function.

4. If the delimiter inserted in the second input has been repeated several times within the reference text, the position of desired repetitions for separation can be determined in this input.

5. If the delimiter inserted in the third input has been repeated several times within the reference text, you can determine in which repetition the separation should end by using the fifth input of this function.

Based on the function explanations, the result of the following formula is equal to the text between the "-" character (its first repetition) and the "/" character (its first repetition), which is equal to "11-181":

```
= Text.BetweenDelimiters(

"XNW-11-181/MN-12/2-",

"-",

"/")
```

To start a separation from the second repetition of "-", you just need to enter the number 1 in the fourth input of this function as follows, so the result of the formula is "181":

```
= Text.BetweenDelimiters(

"XNW-11-181/MN-12/2-",

"-",

"/",

1)
```

Similarly, if the number 1 is also entered in the fifth input of this function, the separation operation will continue until the second repetition of "/" and the result will be equal to "181/MN-12".

```
= Text.BetweenDelimiters(

"XNW-11-181/MN-12/2-",

"-",
```

```
"/",

1,

1)
```

It should be noted that like the previous functions, to determine the direction of finding the delimiters in the fourth and fifth inputs, `RelativePosition.FromStart` and `RelativePosition.FromEnd` can be used beside the number in the list format.

Text.Select

To extract special characters from a reference text, `Text.Select` can be used as follows:

```
Text.Select(
        text as nullable text,
        selectChars as any
              ) as nullable text
```

This function receives two arguments.

1. The reference text is entered in the first argument.

2. The characters or list of characters for extracting are entered in the second input in the format of a text or a list of texts. Entering "XZ" in this input respectively means extracting all the XZ in the reference text, but entering {"X", "Z"} means extracting all the X or Z in the reference text.

So, by the following formula, all the repetition of characters "2", "X", and "-" should be extracted from the reference text entered in the first input, and the result is equal to "22-X-2":

```
= Text.Select("2023-YXL-12",{"2","X","-"})
```

In the next example, all uppercase alphabetic characters should be extracted from the reference text, and the result is equal to "YXL".

```
= Text.Select("2023-YXL-12",{"A".."Z"})
```

Text.Split

Text.Split is used to split a reference text into several texts based on a delimiter. For example, "X-12-M81" can be divided into {"X", "12", "M81"} by this function (in this case, the delimiter is "-"):

```
Text.Split(
        text as text,
        separator as text
                ) as list
```

This function takes the following two arguments and results in a list of separated texts:

1. The reference text is entered in the first argument.

2. The second argument represents the character or characters that act as the delimiter for splitting the text. Entering the "-" in this input means that the parts of the reference text after "-" should be split.

Various examples of this function are listed in Table 4-7.

Table 4-7. *Examples of Text.Split*

Formula	Result
= Text.Split("XNW-11-181-M","-")	{"XNW","11","181","M"}
= Text.Split("XNW-11-181-M","1")	}"XNW-","","-","8","-M"}
= Text.Split("XNW-11-181-M","n")	}"XNW-11-181-M"}
= Text.Split("XNW-11-181-M","N")	}"X","W-11-181-M"}

In the same way, Text.SplitAny can be used to split a reference text based on each repetition of single characters inserted in the second argument. So the result of the following formula is {"XN","","11","181","M"}, while using Text.Split results in {"XN","11-181-M"}:

```
= Text.SplitAny("XNW-11-181-M","W-")
```

Removing, Replacing, and Combining Texts

In this section, the functions for removing a part of a text or replacing it with new characters or combining different texts are explained.

Text.Remove

Specific characters can be removed from a reference text by using Text. Remove as follows.

```
Text.Remove(
        text as nullable text,
        removeChars as any
            ) as nullable text
```

This function takes these two inputs:

1. The first input is the reference text.

2. The second input defines the characters that you want to remove from the reference text. To remove a character or substring, it can be entered as a text in this input, but to remove several characters or substrings, they should be entered as a list within {}.

Table 4-8 provides various examples of this function.

Table 4-8. *Examples of Text.Remove*

Formula	Result
= Text.Remove("XNW-11-181/MN","1")	"XNW--8/MN"
= Text.Remove("XNW-11-181/MN","-")	"XNW11181/MN"
= Text.Remove("XNW-11-181/MN","/")	"XNW-11-181MN"
= Text.Remove("XNW-11-181/MN",{"1","-","/"})	"XNW8MN"
= Text.Remove("XNW-11-181/MN",{"A".."Z"})	"-11-181/"

In another case, by using the following formula, all numbers within the reference text can be removed. In this case, the result of the formula is equal to "XNW--/MN".

```
= Text.Remove("XNW-11-181/MN",{"0".."9"})
```

By using the following formula, all capital letters in the text can be removed. In this case, the result of the formula is equal to " -11-181/ ".

```
= Text.Remove("XNW-11-181/MN",{"A".."Z"})
```

In another example, by using the following formula, all letters within the text can be removed:

```
= Text.Remove("XNW-11-181/MN",{"a".."z","A".."Z"})
```

Text.RemoveRange

The Text.RemoveRange function is used to remove a sequence of characters in the reference text based on their position (for example, removing the seventh to tenth characters within a specific text). This function is defined in Power Query as follows:

```
Text.RemoveRange(
text as nullable text,
offset as number,
optional count as nullable number
        ) as nullable text
```

Text.RemoveRange takes three arguments:

1. The reference text is defined in the first argument.

2. The starting position for removing is determined in the second argument. (Note that positions start from 0.)

3. In the third argument, the number of characters to be removed is entered. This input is optional, and if no value is entered, the number 1 is considered.

To better examine this function, multiple examples are provided in Table 4-9.

Table 4-9. *Examples of Text.RemoveRange*

Formula	Result
= Text.RemoveRange("2023-YXL-12",0,5)	"YXL-12"
= Text.RemoveRange("2023-YXL-12",4,5)	"202312"
= Text.RemoveRange("2023-YXL-12",8,3)	"YXL-12"
= Text.RemoveRange("2023-YXL-12",8,5)	Error

Text.PadEnd

By using Text.PadEnd, the length of a text (number of characters) can be increased to the desired number and new spaces can be filled with a specified character at the end of the text.

```
Text.PadEnd(
        text as nullable text,
        count as number,
        optional character as nullable text
                ) as nullable text
```

This function takes three inputs as follows:

1. The first input of this function represents the reference text.

2. In the second input, the length of output is determined by entering a number.

3. In this input, the desired character(s) for filling the empty spaces is determined. This input is optional; if not entered, the space will be considered instead.

According to the above explanation, based on the following formula, the output must contain five characters and the empty spaces at the end of the reference text must be filled with "X". Therefore, the result is "AWXXX".

```
= Text.PadEnd("AW",5,"X")
```

Based on the function explanations, various examples of this function are given in Table 4-10.

Table 4-10. *Examples of Text.PadEnd*

Formula	Result
= Text.PadEnd("AW",5,"X")	"AWXXX"
= Text.PadEnd("AW",5)	"AW "
= Text.PadEnd("AW",1,"X")	"AW"

Text.PadStart

The Text.PadStart function is like the Text.PadEnd function. The difference is that in this function, the desired character will be placed at the beginning of the reference text. In other words, by using Text. PadStart, the length of a text can be increased by repeating new character(s) at the beginning of it. This function is defined as follows:

```
Text.PadStart(
    text as nullable text,
    count as number,
    optional character as nullable text
        ) as nullable text
```

This function has three inputs as follows:

1. The first input of this function represents the reference text.

2. The desired length of output text is specified in the second input.

3. In the third input, the desired character(s) for filling the empty spaces is entered.

Based on the function explanations, various examples of this function are listed in Table 4-11.

Table 4-11. *Examples of Text.PadStart*

Formula	Result
= Text.PadStart("AW",5,"X")	"XXXAW"
= Text.PadStart("AW",5)	" AW"
= Text.PadStart("AW",1,"X")	"AW"

Text.Replace

By using this function, a substring in a text can be replaced with new characters as follows:

```
Text.Replace(
        text as nullable text,
        old as text,
        new as text
              ) as nullable text
```

This function takes the following three arguments:

1. The reference text is entered in the first input.

2. The substring that should be removed and replaced by new characters is entered in this input.

3. The new text that should replace the deleted part is defined in the third input.

Using this function, the substring entered in the second input is replaced with the text specified in the third input in the reference text. Table 4-12 shows some applications of this function.

Table 4-12. *Examples of Text.Replace*

Formula	Result
= Text.Replace("XNW-11-181/MN","-","/")	"XNW/11/181/MN"
= Text.Replace("XNW-11-181/MN","/","-")	"XNW-11-181-MN"
= Text.Replace("XNW-11-181/MN","XNW","U")	"U-11-181/MN"

Text.ReplaceRange

Text.ReplaceRange is used to replace several characters with new characters based on their position in the reference text. This function is defined in the following way in Power Query:

```
Text.ReplaceRange(
        text as nullable text,
        offset as number,
        count as number,
        newText as text
                ) as nullable text
```

.

This function takes four arguments as follows:

1. The first argument represents the reference text.

2. The starting point for deletion from the reference text is determined in the second argument by entering a number.

3. The third input of this function represents the number of characters you want to remove from the reference text.

4. The substitute text is defined in this input.

Based on the above description, by the following formula, the three characters after the sixth (5+1) character are replaced by "A" and the result is equal to "2023-A-12".

```
= Text.RemoveRange("2023-YXL-12",5,3,"A")
```

Text.Insert

To add new characters to the reference text, Text.Insert is used as follows:

```
Text.Insert(
        text as nullable text,
        offset as number,
        newText as text
        ) as nullable text
```

This function takes the following three inputs:

1. The reference text is entered as the first input.

2. In the second input, the position of adding the new text is determined.

3. Finally, in the third input of this function, the text or characters for adding to the reference text is determined.

Table 4-13 shows several examples of this function.

Table 4-13. *Examples of Text.Insert*

Formula	Result
= Text.Insert("2023-YXL-12",0,"AB-")	"AB-2023-YXL-12"
= Text.Insert("2023-YXL-12",5,"AB-")	"2023-AB-YXL-12"
= Text.Insert("2023-YXL-12",9,"AB-")	"2023-YXL-AB-12"

Text.Repeat

The Text.Repeat function is used to repeat a text as desired numbers, as follows:

```
Text.Repeat(
     text as nullable text,
     count as number
     ) as nullable text
```

This function receives two inputs as follows:

1. In the first input of this function, the text is entered.

2. The repetition count is specified in the second input by entering a number.

Considering the function explanations, the result of this function for different values is listed in Table 4-14.

Table 4-14. *Examples of Text.Repeat*

Formula	Result
= Text.Repeat("X",3)	"XXX"
= Text.Repeat("X-",3)	"X-X-X-"
= Text.Repeat("X-Y",3)	"X-YX-YX-Y"

Text.Combine

By using Text.Combine, two or more texts can be combined and result in a text.

```
Text.Combine(
     texts as list,
     optional separator as nullable text
          ) as text
```

This function takes two arguments as follows:

1. In the first argument, a list of texts to combine is entered.

2. The separator is determined in the second argument. This input is optional; if no separator is entered, it will not be considered.

Table 4-15 provides various examples of this function.

Table 4-15. *Examples of Text.Combine*

Formula	Result
= Text.Combine({"A","B","C"})	"ABC"
= Text.Combine({"A","B","C"},"-")	"A-B-C"
= Text.Combine({"A","B","C"}," ")	"A B C"

Text Correction

There are various functions in Power Query to modify texts. These functions mostly receive a text as input and, after removing extra spaces, special characters, and capitalizing or lowercasing letters in the reference text, display the corrected text as output. Table 4-16 lists these functions along with their application.

Table 4-16. *List of Text Correction Functions*

Functions	Description
Text.Lower*	Using this function, all English letters in the inputed text will be converted to lowercase.
Text.Upper*	The output of this function will be the same as the input text, except that all letters in the output will be displayed in uppercase.
Text.Proper*	The output of this function will be the same as the input text, except that in the output text, the first letter of all words will be displayed in uppercase, and the other letters will be displayed in lowercase.
Text.Reverse	Using this function, the sequence of characters in the reference text will be reversed.
Text.Trim*	Using this function, all extra spaces in a text (spaces at the beginning, ending, or spaces next to each other) can be removed.
Text.TrimEnd*	Using this function, extra spaces at the end of the text can be removed.
Text.TrimStart*	Using this function, extra spaces at the beginning of the text can be removed.
Text.Clean	Using this function, special characters such as #(if) within the text can be removed, in addition to extra spaces.
Text.Length	This function is used to determine the number of characters in the reference text.

Table 4-17 lists several examples of these functions.

Table 4-17. *Examples of Text Correction Functions*

Formula	Result
=Text.Lower("MN-12qw sx")	"mn-12qw sx"
=Text.Upper("MN-12qw sx")	"MN-12QW SX"
=Text.Lower("MN-12qw sx")	"Mn-12Qw Sx"
= Text.Trim(" WS mn- 1 ")	"WS mn- 1"
= Text.TrimStart(" WS mn- 1 ")	"WS mn- 1 "
= Text.TrimEnd(" WS mn- 1 ")	" WS mn- 1"
= Text.TrimEnd(" WS mn- 1 X X ",{" ","X"})	" WS mn- 1"

Searching for Characters

In this section, different functions to search for a specific character in the reference text are described. These functions are divided into two groups. In the first group, the function will result in True or False, while in the second group, the position of the searching characters in the reference text will be displayed as output.

Text.StartsWith

To check the initial characters of a text, Text.StartsWith can be used as follows:

```
Text.StartsWith(
        text as nullable text,
        substring as text,
        optional comparer as nullable function
                ) as nullable logical
```

Using this function, you can check whether a text starts with certain characters or not. This function takes three arguments as follows, and its output is always True or False.

1. The reference text is entered in the first argument.

2. The substring that you want to compare the initial characters of the reference text to are entered in the second input.

3. This input is optional and determines the comparison logic. If this input is not entered, the function is sensitive to uppercase and lowercase letters. Entering the expression `Comparer.OrdinalIgnoreCase` means the function is no longer sensitive to uppercase and lowercase letters. The different cases of this input are as follows:

   `Comparer.Equals`

   `Comparer.FromCulture`

   `Comparer.Ordinal`

   `Comparer.OrdinalIgnoreCase`

Based on the above explanations, different examples of using this function are provided in Table 4-18.

Table 4-18. *Examples of Text.StartsWith*

Formula	Result
= Text.StartsWith("XN18-M13","X")	True
= Text.StartsWith("XN18-M13","XN1")	True
= Text.StartsWith("XN18-M13","xn")	False
= Text.StartsWith("XN18-M13","xn", Comparer.OrdinalIgnoreCase)	True

Text.EndsWith

To examine the ending characters of a text, `Text.EndsWith` can be used as follows:

```
Text.EndsWith(
        text as nullable text,
        substring as text,
        optional comparer as nullable function
                ) as nullable logical
```

By using this function, you can check whether a text ends with certain characters or not. This function receives the following three inputs, and its output is always equal to True or False.

1. The reference text.

2. The desired characters that you want to compare with the ending characters of the reference text.

3. This input is optional and determines the comparison logic, and its different cases are

    `Comparer.Equals`

    `Comparer.FromCulture`

    `Comparer.Ordinal`

    `Comparer.OrdinalIgnoreCase`

Based on the above explanations, different examples of using this function are provided in Table 4-19.

Table 4-19. Examples of Text.EndsWith

Formula	Result
= Text.EndsWith("XN18-M13","M13")	True
= Text.EndsWith("XN18-M13","13")	True
= Text.EndsWith("XN18-M13","m13")	False
= Text.EndsWith("XN18-M13","m13", Comparer. OrdinalIgnoreCase)	True

Text.Contains

To check the existence of substring in a reference text, Text.Contains can be used as follows:

```
Text.Contains(
        text as nullable text,
        substring as text,
        optional comparer as nullable function
            ) as nullable logical
```

This function takes these three below inputs:

1. The first input is the reference text.

2. The substring that you want to search for in the reference text is entered in the second input.

3. This input is optional and determines the comparison logic. If this input is not entered, the function is case-sensitive. Entering the expression Comparer.OrdinalIgnoreCase means the function

is no longer case-sensitive. The different cases for this input are

```
Comparer.Equals
```

```
Comparer.FromCulture
```

```
Comparer.Ordinal
```

```
Comparer.OrdinalIgnoreCase
```

Based on the function explanations, the result of this function for different examples is given in Table 4-20.

Table 4-20. *Examples of Text.Contains*

Formula	Result
= Text.Contains("XN18-M13","M")	True
= Text.Contains("XN18-M13","8-M")	True
= Text.Contains("XN18-M13","m")	False
= Text.Contains("XN18-M13","M", Comparer.OrdinalIgnoreCase)	True

Text.PositionOf

To obtain the position of a substring in the reference text, Text. PositionOf can be used as follows:

```
Text.PositionOf(
        text as text,
        substring as text,
        optional occurrence as nullable number,
        optional comparer as nullable function
            ) as any
```

This function has the four following inputs:

1. The first input is the reference text.

2. The second input is a substring that you want to search for in the reference text.

3. If the entered substring from the second input is repeated more than once in the reference text, the desired position is determined in this input by entering numbers 0, 1, or 2 or by using the expressions Occurrence.First, Occurrence.Last, or Occurrence. All. This input is optional, and its default value is 0.

4. The logic of comparing the substring is determined in this input. This input is optional, and its default state is case-sensitive, but entering Comparer. OrdinalIgnoreCase in this input means that it is not case-sensitive. The different states of this input are

Comparer.Equals

Comparer.FromCulture

Comparer.Ordinal

Comparer.OrdinalIgnoreCase

In Table 4-21, numerous examples of this function are provided.

Table 4-21. *Examples of Text.PositionOf*

Formula	Result
= Text.PositionOf("XNW-11-181-M","-")	3
= Text.PositionOf("XNW-11-181-M","-",1)	10
= Text.PositionOf("XNW-11-181-M","-", Occurrence.Last)	10
= Text.PositionOf("XNW-11-181-M","-",2)	{3,6,10}
= Text.PositionOf("XNW-11-181-M","R")	-1

Text.PositionOfAny

Text.PositionOfAny is like Text.PositionOf. The difference is that using Text.PositionOfAny means it's possible to simultaneously search for multiple strings within the reference text, as follows:

```
Text.PositionOfAny(
    text as text,
    characters as list,
    optional occurrence as nullable number
        ) as any
```

This function takes these three inputs:

1. The reference text.

2. The second input is in the form of a list and contains the substrings for which you want to find the positions in the reference text.

3. This input is optional. By entering the numbers 0, 1, or 2, you specify whether the smallest number (first repetition at the beginning of the text), the largest number (last repetition at the end of the text), or all numbers should be displayed in the output.

Table 4-22 provides examples of this function.

Table 4-22. *Examples of Text.PositionOfAny*

Formula	Result
= Text.PositionOfAny("XNW-11-181-M",{"-"})	3
= Text.PositionOfAny("XNW-11-181-M",{"1"})	4
= Text.PositionOfAny("XNW-11-181-M",{"-","1"})	3
= Text.PositionOfAny("XNW-11-181-M",{"-","1"},1)	10
= Text.PositionOfAny("XNW-11-181-M",{"-","1"},2)	{3,4,5,6,7,9,10}

Text Conversion

In Power Query, the format of values is important, and each function works on a specific range of formats. For example, in the first input of Text.Start, a text must be entered, and entering a number will result in an error. So, to separate the first four characters (year) in the number 20231123, firstly it should be converted to text and then you can perform the desired operation on it.

There are different functions in Power Query for values format conversion, which are explained in Table 4-23.

Table 4-23. *Text Conversion Functions*

Function	Description
Character.FromNumber	This function receives a number (ASCII code) as input and displays the corresponding character in the output.
Character.ToNumber	This function receives a character as input and displays the corresponding ASCII code in the output.
Text.From	This function receives a number as input and displays the same number in text format in the output.
Text.ToList	This function receives a text as input, separates each character of the number, and displays the result as a list in the output.
Value.FromText	This function receives a number in text format as input and displays the same number in a numerical format in the output.

Table 4-24 shows the results of these functions.

Table 4-24. *Examples of Text Conversion Functions*

Formula	Result
Character.FromNumber(65)	"A"
Character.ToNumber("A")	65
Text.From(83)	"83"
Text.ToList("Hello")	{"H","e","L","L","O"}
Value.FromText("83")	83

Summary

In this chapter, you embarked on a journey through the world of text functions within Power Query, unveiling a toolkit that empowers data professionals to conquer the complexities of unstructured and semi-structured text data. Textual information, from customer feedback to product descriptions, is integral to our digital lives, and mastering its manipulation is essential for data transformation.

You began by understanding the fundamentals of text encoding, manipulation, and the role of Power Query's text functions in these processes. You explored the art of efficiently extracting specific elements from strings, a skill that allows you to isolate URLs from paragraphs or capture dates from lengthy narratives.

Moving forward, you delved into techniques for cleansing and standardizing data, including removing extraneous spaces, punctuation, and converting case formats. These operations form the foundation of consistent and reliable text analysis.

To complete the Power Query functions, the functions related to manipulating the dates and times are presented in the next chapter. These functions are used to extract the required information from the values in the format of time and date. So you will learn how to add or subtract specific values from dates or how to compare the different date values.

CHAPTER 5

Date and Time Functions

In the ever-evolving landscape of data analysis and manipulation, time stands as an unyielding dimension. From sales records stamped with precise transaction times to project timelines meticulously tracked, understanding and harnessing the intricate world of dates and times is essential. This chapter delves into the realm of Power Query's date and time functions, illuminating the path to conquering temporal data complexities with finesse and accuracy.

Dates and times are more than mere numbers on a screen; they represent the pulse of business operations, the rhythm of customer behaviors, and the progression of events. Yet these timestamps are often fragmented, inconsistent, or divergent across data sources. Power Query, with its arsenal of specialized functions, offers the key to harmonizing and unlocking the insights hidden within temporal data.

Your expedition begins with an exploration of foundational concepts, dispelling the mystique surrounding date and time formats. Understanding the subtleties of international standards, time zones, and date arithmetic is paramount to effective temporal data manipulation.

As you delve deeper, you'll encounter the power of date and time functions in transforming raw timestamps into intelligible and meaningful information. From extracting day-of-week patterns to calculating the

© Omid Motamedisedeh 2024
O. Motamedisedeh, *The Ultimate Guide to Functions in Power Query*,
https://doi.org/10.1007/978-1-4842-9754-4_5

duration between critical milestones, these functions serve as the building blocks of temporal analysis.

The initial function, `DateTime.LocalNow`, without any argument, can be used as follows to determine date of today and time of now:

```
DateTime.LocalNow() as datetime
```

Date Information

To examine if a date is in a specific date period (such as last week or next month) or not, several functions can be used. The following is a list of the functions you can use to examine the availability of a date in the next, previous, or current time period (just one time period):

Date.IsInCurrentDay	Date.IsInPreviousDay	Date.IsInNextDay
Date.IsInCurrentWeek	Date.IsInPreviousWeek	Date.IsInNextWeek
Date.IsInCurrentMonth	Date.IsInPreviousMonth	Date.IsInNextMonth
Date.IsInCurrentQuarter	Date.IsInPreviousQuarter	Date.IsInNextQuarter
Date.IsInCurrentYear	Date.IsInPreviousYear	Date.IsInNextYear

All of the above functions take an argument in the format of a date. Based on the entered value, comparing it with the value of `DateTime.LocalNow()`, the function result will be true or false. For example, the `Date.IsInCurrentMonth` indicates whether the given datetime value occurs during the current month (determined by the current date and time on the system) or not.

The above-mentioned functions are used to evaluate the availability of a date in the next or previous time period (they can used for check the availability of a date in the next month but not the next two month), but to examine if a date is in more than one next or previous time periods (N times period), one of the following functions can be used:

Date.IsInPreviousNDays   Date.IsInNextNDays

Date.IsInPreviousNWeeks   Date.IsInNextNWeeks

Date.IsInPreviousNMonths   Date.IsInNextNMonths

Date.IsInPreviousNQuarters   Date.IsInNextNQuarters

Date.IsInPreviousNYears   Date.IsInNextNYears

All of the above mentioned functions take two arguments:

1. The date value is entered as the first argument.

2. The N, as the number of the next or previous period, is determined in the second argument.

So the result of Date.IsInPreviousNYears(X,2) is true, if X is a date in the period of the last two years.

Assuming that today's date is April 14, 2023, the results of different formulas in this group are shown in Table 5-1. (To save space, the expression Date.IsIn has been removed from the beginning of all functions names; True is represented by T; False is represented by F; and x represents the dates entered in the column titles.)

Table 5-1. Date Information Functions

Reference Date (x)	5/03/2023	18/12/2022	12/10/2023	18/04/2023	18/08/2023	19/02/2023	15/06/2023	1/02/2023	4/09/2023	11/02/2022	10/09/2022	9/03/2024	24/07/2022	22/04/2022	24/05/2022	11/10/2022	4/11/2023	18/11/2022
CurrentMonth(x)	F	F	F	T	F	F	F	F	F	F	F	F	F	F	F	F	F	F
NextMonth(x)	F	F	F	F	F	F	F	F	F	F	F	F	F	F	F	F	T	F
PreviousMonth(x)	T	F	F	F	F	F	F	F	F	F	F	F	F	F	F	F	F	F
NextYear(x)	F	F	F	F	F	F	F	F	F	F	F	T	F	F	F	F	F	F
CurrentYear(x)	T	F	T	T	T	T	T	T	T	F	F	F	F	F	F	F	F	F
NextNQuarters(x,5)	F	F	T	F	T	F	F	F	T	F	F	T	F	F	F	F	T	F
PreviousQuarter(x)	T	F	F	F	F	T	F	T	F	F	F	F	F	F	F	F	F	F
NextNMonths(x,7)	F	F	T	F	T	T	T	F	T	F	F	F	F	F	F	F	T	F
CurrentWeek(x)	F	F	F	F	F	F	F	F	F	F	F	F	F	F	F	F	F	F

DateTime Information

Like the functions in the previous section, this group of information functions also includes two groups. The first group of functions, including the following functions, receives one input and is used to check the existence of an entered time in the input during a time (hour, minute, or second) before or after the current time. The following cases are included:

DateTime.IsInCurrentHour

DateTime.IsInCurrentMinute

DateTime.IsInCurrentSecond

DateTime.IsInNextHour

DateTime.IsInNextMinute

DateTime.IsInNextSecond

DateTime.IsInNextNHours

DateTime.IsInNextNMinutes

DateTime.IsInNextNSeconds

The second group of functions receives two inputs (date and time to be checked and N as the number of time periods) and are used to check the existence of a time in N time periods (hour, minute, or second) before or after the current time. The functions in this group are as follows:

DateTime.IsInPreviousHour

DateTime.IsInPreviousMinute

DateTime.IsInPreviousNHours

DateTime.IsInPreviousNMinutes

Assuming that the current time is 4:30 on April 14, 2023, the result of various formulas is shown in Table 5-2. (To shorten the table, the phrase DateTime.IsIn has been removed from the beginning of all functions, and the term X is used instead of the date and time value.)

Table 5-2. *Datetime Information Functions*

Reference Date (x)	Current Hour(X)	Next Hour(X)	Previous Hour(X)	NextN Minutes (X,120)	Previous NHours (X,12)
13/04/2023 19:36	FALSE	FALSE	FALSE	FALSE	FALSE
12/04/2023 16:47	FALSE	FALSE	FALSE	FALSE	FALSE
13/04/2023 13:47	FALSE	FALSE	FALSE	FALSE	FALSE
14/04/2023 16:41	TRUE	FALSE	FALSE	TRUE	FALSE
12/04/2023 17:32	FALSE	FALSE	FALSE	FALSE	FALSE
12/04/2023 17:49	FALSE	FALSE	FALSE	FALSE	FALSE
14/04/2023 4:32	FALSE	FALSE	FALSE	FALSE	TRUE
13/04/2023 8:49	FALSE	FALSE	FALSE	FALSE	FALSE
13/04/2023 22:48	FALSE	FALSE	FALSE	FALSE	FALSE
13/04/2023 2:45	FALSE	FALSE	FALSE	FALSE	FALSE
12/04/2023 22:29	FALSE	FALSE	FALSE	FALSE	FALSE
12/04/2023 4:23	FALSE	FALSE	FALSE	FALSE	FALSE
13/04/2023 7:47	FALSE	FALSE	FALSE	FALSE	FALSE
14/04/2023 3:23	FALSE	FALSE	FALSE	FALSE	FALSE
12/04/2023 2:10	FALSE	FALSE	FALSE	FALSE	FALSE
14/04/2023 8:07	FALSE	FALSE	FALSE	FALSE	TRUE
13/04/2023 0:08	FALSE	FALSE	FALSE	FALSE	FALSE
13/04/2023 17:01	FALSE	FALSE	FALSE	FALSE	FALSE

Adding a Value to a Date

In Power Query, several functions can be used to add or subtract a certain number of days, weeks, months, seasons, or years to a date. These functions, which are described below, receive two inputs. The first input is the reference date and the second input is a value in number format (positive or negative) to determine the number of days, weeks, months, quarters, or years you want to add to (if the entered value is positive) or subtract from (if the entered value is negative) the reference date. This group includes the following functions:

Date.AddDays(**dateTime** as any, **numberOfDays** as number) as any

Date.AddMonths(**dateTime** as any, **numberOfMonths** as number) as any

Date.AddQuarters(**dateTime** as any, **numberOfQuarters** as number) as any

Date.AddWeeks(**dateTime** as any, **numberOfWeeks** as number) as any

Date.AddYears(**dateTime** as any, **numberOfYears** as number) as any

According to the function explanations, the results of these functions for different examples are as shown in Table 5-3. (The first parameter of all formulas, which is in date type, has been entered in the first column of Table 5-3 and is shown by x in the formulas).

Table 5-3. *Adding To or Subtracting From Dates*

Reference Date (x)	AddDays (x,2)	AddDays (x,-5)	AddMonths (x,-3)	Addyears (x,-2)
31/03/2023	2/04/2023	26/03/2023	31/12/2022	31/03/2021
5/04/2023	7/04/2023	31/03/2023	5/01/2023	5/04/2021
8/04/2023	10/04/2023	3/04/2023	8/01/2023	8/04/2021

(*continued*)

Table 5-3. (*continued*)

Reference Date (x)	AddDays (x,2)	AddDays (x,-5)	AddMonths (x,-3)	Addyears (x,-2)
12/04/2023	14/04/2023	7/04/2023	12/01/2023	12/04/2021
13/04/2023	15/04/2023	8/04/2023	13/01/2023	13/04/2021
14/04/2023	16/04/2023	9/04/2023	14/01/2023	14/04/2021
16/04/2023	18/04/2023	11/04/2023	16/01/2023	16/04/2021
22/04/2023	24/04/2023	17/04/2023	22/01/2023	22/04/2021
24/04/2023	26/04/2023	19/04/2023	24/01/2023	24/04/2021
28/04/2023	30/04/2023	23/04/2023	28/01/2023	28/04/2021
3/05/2023	5/05/2023	28/04/2023	3/02/2023	3/05/2021
4/05/2023	6/05/2023	29/04/2023	4/02/2023	4/05/2021
9/05/2023	11/05/2023	4/05/2023	9/02/2023	9/05/2021
17/05/2023	19/05/2023	12/05/2023	17/02/2023	17/05/2021
19/05/2023	21/05/2023	14/05/2023	19/02/2023	19/05/2021

Shifting Dates

To determine the start or end date of the week, month, season, or year of a specific date, the following functions can be used:

Date.EndOfDay	Date.StartOfDay
Date.EndOfWeek	Date.StartOfWeek
Date.EndOfMonth	Date.StartOfMonth
Date.EndOfQuarter	Date.StartOfQuarter
Date.EndOfYear	Date.StartOfYear

So, by entering a date in the first argument of Date.EndOfYear, the last date on the year of the date entered in the first argument is shown, and the result of Date.StartOfYear is the first date of that year. See Table 5-4.

Table 5-4. *Shifting Date Functions*

Reference Date	Date. EndOfDay	Date. EndOfWeek	Date. EndOfMonth	Date. EndOfYear
27/07/2020	2/08/2020	31/07/2020	30/09/2020	31/12/2020
30/07/2020	2/08/2020	31/07/2020	30/09/2020	31/12/2020
8/11/2020	8/11/2020	30/11/2020	31/12/2020	31/12/2020
5/01/2021	10/01/2021	31/01/2021	31/03/2021	31/12/2021
8/04/2021	11/04/2021	30/04/2021	30/06/2021	31/12/2021
6/09/2021	12/09/2021	30/09/2021	30/09/2021	31/12/2021
2/10/2021	3/10/2021	31/10/2021	31/12/2021	31/12/2021
19/11/2021	21/11/2021	30/11/2021	31/12/2021	31/12/2021
27/11/2021	28/11/2021	30/11/2021	31/12/2021	31/12/2021
26/12/2021	26/12/2021	31/12/2021	31/12/2021	31/12/2021
14/02/2022	20/02/2022	28/02/2022	31/03/2022	31/12/2022
30/03/2022	3/04/2022	31/03/2022	31/03/2022	31/12/2022
28/04/2022	1/05/2022	30/04/2022	30/06/2022	31/12/2022
12/06/2022	12/06/2022	30/06/2022	30/06/2022	31/12/2022
22/07/2022	24/07/2022	31/07/2022	30/09/2022	31/12/2022
7/11/2022	13/11/2022	30/11/2022	31/12/2022	31/12/2022
24/01/2023	29/01/2023	31/01/2023	31/03/2023	31/12/2023
26/03/2023	26/03/2023	31/03/2023	31/03/2023	31/12/2023

The results of these functions are provided in Table 5-5.

Table 5-5. *Shifting Date Functions*

Reference Date	StartofDay	StartOfWeek	StartOf Month	StartOf Quarter	StartOf Year
27/07/2020	27/07/2020	27/07/2020	1/07/2020	1/07/2020	1/01/2020
30/07/2020	30/07/2020	27/07/2020	1/07/2020	1/07/2020	1/01/2020
8/11/2020	8/11/2020	2/11/2020	1/11/2020	1/10/2020	1/01/2020
5/01/2021	5/01/2021	4/01/2021	1/01/2021	1/01/2021	1/01/2021
8/04/2021	8/04/2021	5/04/2021	1/04/2021	1/04/2021	1/01/2021
6/09/2021	6/09/2021	6/09/2021	1/09/2021	1/07/2021	1/01/2021
2/10/2021	2/10/2021	27/09/2021	1/10/2021	1/10/2021	1/01/2021
19/11/2021	19/11/2021	15/11/2021	1/11/2021	1/10/2021	1/01/2021
27/11/2021	27/11/2021	22/11/2021	1/11/2021	1/10/2021	1/01/2021
26/12/2021	26/12/2021	20/12/2021	1/12/2021	1/10/2021	1/01/2021
14/02/2022	14/02/2022	14/02/2022	1/02/2022	1/01/2022	1/01/2022
30/03/2022	30/03/2022	28/03/2022	1/03/2022	1/01/2022	1/01/2022
28/04/2022	28/04/2022	25/04/2022	1/04/2022	1/04/2022	1/01/2022
12/06/2022	12/06/2022	6/06/2022	1/06/2022	1/04/2022	1/01/2022
22/07/2022	22/07/2022	18/07/2022	1/07/2022	1/07/2022	1/01/2022
7/11/2022	7/11/2022	7/11/2022	1/11/2022	1/10/2022	1/01/2022
24/01/2023	24/01/2023	23/01/2023	1/01/2023	1/01/2023	1/01/2023
26/03/2023	26/03/2023	20/03/2023	1/03/2023	1/01/2023	1/01/2023

Conversion to Record

Several functions can be used to convert date values to the record. The Time.ToRecord, as the initial function, is used to convert a time value as follows to a record:

Time.ToRecord(**Time** as time) as record

Based on the function syntax, it takes an input in the type of time and displays the time values in a record in the output. Therefore, the result of the formula Time.ToRecord(#time(2,10,30)) is equal to the following value:

[Hour=2, Minute=10, Second=30]

Similarly, the Date.ToRecord function is used to convert a date value as follows to a record:

Date.ToRecord(**Date** as date) as record

Based on the function syntax, it takes an input in the format of a date and displays the date values in a record in the output. Therefore, the result of the formula Date.ToRecord(#date(2022,5,3)) is equal to the following value:

[Year=2022, Month=5, Day=3]

Another function in this group is the DateTime.ToRecord, which is used to convert a date and time value to a record. This function takes an input of type datetime and displays its values in a record as output.

DateTime.ToRecord(**DateTime** as datetime) as record

As you can see, this function receives an input and displays its values in a record in the output. Therefore, the result of the formula DateTime.ToR ecord(#datetime(2022,5,3,2,10,30)) is equal to the following value:

[Year=2022, Month=5, Day=3, Hour=2, Minute=10, Second=30]

Date Specifications

There are different functions, described below, in Power Query to extract the information (number of day, month, or year) from date values.

Date.Day

This function is defined as follows in Power Query and takes an input of type date, and in the output, and the day value of the reference date is shown in the result.

```
Date.Day(dateTime as any) as nullable number
```

In other words, this function displays the day part of the entered date in the output. Therefore, the result of the following formula will be equal to the number 3:

```
= Date.Day(#date(2022,5,3))
```

Date.DayOfWeek

Using this function, the day number (in a week) of a date can be determined. This function is defined as follows in Power Query and receives two inputs. The first input is of type date, and in the second input, entering values such as Day.Sunday or Day.Monday, you specify which day of the week is the first day of each week.

```
Date.DayOfWeek(
        dateTime as any,
        optional firstDayOfWeek as nullable number
            ) as nullable number
```

This function always returns a number and represents the day of the week. The result of the following formula is equal to 1:

```
= Date.DayOfWeek(#date(2022,5,3))
```

Date.DayOfWeekName

This function is like the Date.DayOfWeek function, but instead of the day number in the week, the day name will be displayed in the output by this function. This function is defined in Power Query as follows:

```
Date.DayOfWeekName(
date as any,
optional culture as nullable text
        )
```

The first input of this function represents the reference date and in the second input, which is optional, the logic of day naming by entering an expression such as "en-US" can be determined. The result of the following formula is equal to Tuesday:

```
= Date.MonthName(#date(2022,5,3))
```

Date.WeekOfMonth

To determine the week number in a month, the following function can be used:

```
Date.WeekOfMonth(
dateTime as any,
optional firstDayOfWeek as nullable number
        ) as nullable number
```

Based on the function syntax, this function receives two inputs. The first input is of type date and in the second input, entering values such as Day.Sunday or Day.Monday, you specify which day of the week is the first day of the week. According to the function explanations, the result of the following formula is equal to 19, indicating that this date belongs to the second week of the year:

```
= Date.WeekOfYear(#date(2022,5,3))
```

Date.WeekOfYear

To determine the week number (from the beginning of the year) of a date, this function can be used as follows:

```
Date.WeekOfYear(
dateTime as any,
optional firstDayOfWeek as nullable number
        ) as nullable number
```

Based on the function syntax, it takes two inputs. The first input is of type date and in the second input, entering values such as Day.Sunday or Day.Monday, you specify which day of the week is the first day of the week. According to the function explanations, the result of the following formula is equal to 19, indicating that this date belongs to the 19th week of the year:

```
= Date.WeekOfYear(#date(2022,5,3))
```

Date.Month

This function is defined in Power Query as follows and receives one input of type date and specifies the month number of entered date:

```
Date.Month(dateTime as any) as nullable number
```

In other words, this function displays the month section of the entered date in the output. Therefore, the result of the following formula is equal to 5:

```
= Date.Month(#date(2022,5,3))
```

Date.MonthName

This function is like the Date.Month function, but instead of the month number, the month name will be displayed in the output. This function is defined in Power Query as follows:

```
Date.MonthName(
date as any,
optional culture as nullable text
        ) as nullable text
```

The first input of this function represents the reference date and in the second input, which is optional, you can define the logic of the month naming by entering an expression such as "en-US". The result of the following formula is equal to May:

```
= Date.MonthName(#date(2022,5,3))
```

Date.DayOfYear

This function is defined in Power Query as follows and receives one input of type date and specifies in the output the day number of the entered date since the beginning of the year:

```
Date.DayOfYear(dateTime as any) as nullable number
```

Therefore, the result of the following formula is 123, indicating that this date belongs to the 123rd day of the year:

```
= Date.DayOfYear(#date(2022,5,3))
```

Date.Year

This function is defined in Power Query as follows. It receives one input of type date and the year value of the entered date will determine in the output.

```
Date.Year(dateTime as any) as nullable number
```

In other words, this function displays the year section of the entered a date in the output. Therefore, the result of the following formula is equal to 2022:

```
= Date.Year(#date(2022,5,3))
```

Summary

In this chapter, you embarked on a journey to master the intricacies of the date and time functions within Power Query. In the realm of data analysis, time is an essential dimension that requires precision and finesse to manipulate effectively.

Your journey began with a deep dive into foundational concepts, such as the nuances of date encoding, time zones, and arithmetic. Armed with this knowledge, you explored the power of date and time functions in transforming raw timestamps into intelligible and meaningful information.

As you ventured further, you discovered how these functions facilitate the extraction of day-of-week patterns, calculations of durations between significant events, and standardization of temporal data formats. This laid the groundwork for effective temporal analysis.

In the next chapter, you'll explore a wide range of functions to manipulate list values. Based on these functions, you can easily generate different lists, filter and sort the values in a list, extract a specific value from a list, or combine lists.

CHAPTER 6

List Functions

In the vast landscape of data manipulation, individual data points often weave together to create a larger narrative. This is where the power of lists comes into play. From collections of sales transactions to arrays of survey responses, lists capture the essence of data relationships and dependencies. Welcome to a chapter dedicated to exploring the realm of list functions within Power Query. They are your gateway to unraveling intricate data structures and unleashing the true potential of interconnected information.

Lists are the threads that weave the fabric of data stories. Imagine dissecting an order into its constituent products, tracking a project's multi-step workflow, or comprehending the dynamics of customer preferences. These scenarios demand the mastery of list functions, the tools that empower data professionals to manipulate, dissect, and reassemble data in ways that were once intricate challenges.

Your journey through this chapter begins with a foundational understanding of lists as versatile data structures. You'll explore their unique properties, from their ordered nature to the ability to hold heterogeneous data types. With this knowledge in hand, you'll plunge into the world of list creation, from the manual assembly of elements to dynamic generation through calculated expressions.

But lists don't merely exist in isolation; they interact, transform, and adapt. You'll explore the arsenal of list functions that Power Query offers to reshape data collections to your exact specifications. Whether it's

© Omid Motamedisedeh 2024
O. Motamedisedeh, *The Ultimate Guide to Functions in Power Query*,
https://doi.org/10.1007/978-1-4842-9754-4_6

filtering elements based on specific criteria, sorting to reveal patterns, or merging lists to stitch together disjointed information, you'll emerge with a newfound appreciation for the art of data manipulation.

Defining a List in Power Query

To create a list, you can easily insert the values between { } and separate them from each other with a comma or use related functions. To define a list of numbers from 1 to 5, it is sufficient to enter the following expression in the formula bar. The result is as shown in Figure 6-1.

```
={1,2,3,4,5}
```

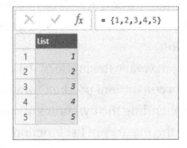

Figure 6-1. *List of numbers from 1 to 5*

To define a list of characters, the following formula can be used. The result is as shown in Figure 6-2.

```
={"a","b","c"}
```

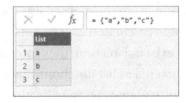

Figure 6-2. *Definition of a list of characters*

To create a list of numbers (e.g., numbers 1 to 100), instead of registering all the numbers between { }, you can enter the initial number following by two dots and the last number. In this case, the entire set of numbers in the corresponding list will be defined. See Figure 6-3.

```
={1..100}
```

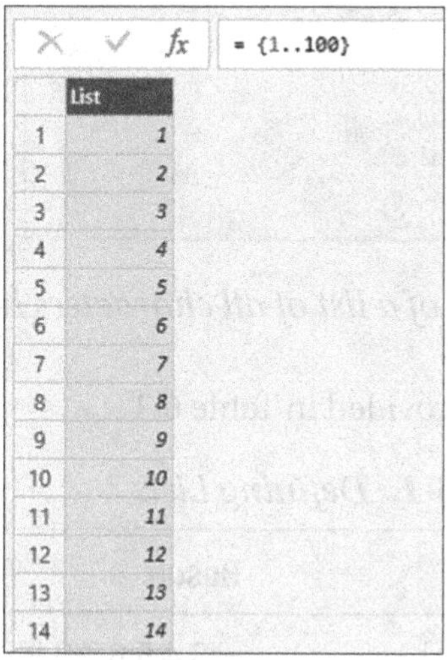

Figure 6-3. *Definition of numbers 1 to 100*

This method is not only for numbers. Characters between c and n can easily defined as follows and as shown in Figure 6-4:

```
= {"c".."n"}
```

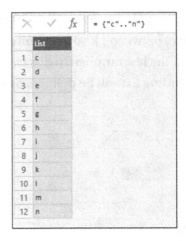

Figure 6-4. *Definition of a list of all characters between c and n*

Some formulas are provided in Table 6-1.

Table 6-1. *Defining Lists*

Formula	Result
= {3..9}	={3,4,5,6,7,8,9}
= {"w","z"}	= {"w","z"}
= {"w".."z"}	={"w","x","y","z"}
= {"W".."Z"}	={"W","X","Y","Z"}
= {"#".."&"}	= {"#","^","%","&"}

In addition to defining a list directly, it is possible to extract values from a column in a table to create a list. In fact, each column of a table represents a list of values (numbers, text, etc.). To extract a column of a table as a list, it is sufficient to enter the name of the table and the column name within square brackets, []. For example, consider TableA (shown in Table 6-2).

Table 6-2. *TableA*

Product	Price	Material
W11	100	Metal
S06	75	Wood
R08	125	Glass

The result of the formula TableA[Price] is equal to a list, including {100,75,12} and the result of the formula TableA[Product] is equal to the list of product names in the form of {"W11", "S06", "R08"}.

Additionally, to create a list, List.Numbers, List.Generate, and other functions can also be used as follows.

List.Numbers

List.Numbers is used as follows to generate a list consisting series of numbers with specific intervals:

```
List.Numbers(
        start as number,
        count as number,
        optional increment as nullable number
            ) as list
```

As observed, this function takes three numerical argument and always returns a list of numbers.

1. The first input represents the initial number of the list.

2. The length of the list is determined in the second input.

3. The third input represents the interval between the numbers in the list. If not entered, the number 1 is considered for this input.

Based on the function explanation, the result of this function is shown in Table 6-3.

Table 6-3. *Examples for List.Numbers*

Formula	Result
= List.Numbers(3,4)	{3,4,5,6}
= List.Numbers(3,4,-1)	{3,2,1,0}
= List.Numbers(3,4,6)	{3,9,15,21}

List.Generate

List.Generate is used as follows to create a list (including numbers, texts, records, or tables):

```
List.Generate(
        initial as function,
        condition as function,
        next as function,
        optional selector as nullable function
            ) as list
```

List.Generate takes four arguments. All are functions, and the last argument is optional.

1. The first argument represents the initial number of the list (in the type of function).

2. The stopping condition for generating values in the list is defined in the second argument (in the type of function).

104

3. In this argument, the formula for generating new value in the list is determined (in the type of function).

4. This input is optional and is known as the selector. With this input, the result of function can be modified.

Let's start with a simple example that represents a list of even numbers less than 10. This function can be defined as follows:

```
= List.Generate(()=>0, (x)=>x< 10, (x)=>x+2)
```

In the first input, the first value is 0. Based on the second input, all values in the list should be lower than 10 (generating values in the list will continue until reaching a value greater than or equal to 10). In the third input, in each iteration, the new value of the list is generated based on the previous value added by 2. This input is a function that receives x as input and results in x+2 as output, in which => is the function sign.

Based on the above example, the desired list starts with the number 0, and in each step, 2 is added to the previous number, and this process continues until you reach the number greater than or equal to 10. Therefore, the result of this formula is {0,2,4,6,8}. See Figure 6-5.

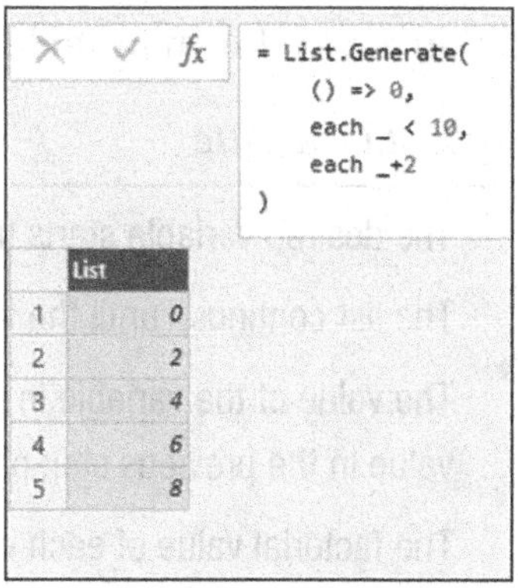

Figure 6-5. Creating even numbers using List.Generate

In the previous example, the variable of x can be replaced by _, so the formula will change to the following:

```
= List.Generate((()=>0, (_)=>_< 10, (_)=>_+2)
```

In this case, the (_)=> can be replaced by each expression as follows:

```
= List.Generate(() =>0, each _ < 10, each _+2)
```

The inputs of this function are themselves type functions, and their explanation is shown in Table 6-4.

Table 6-4. *Parameters of List.Generate*

() =>0,	In this input, it is specified that the list starts with the number 0.
each < 10,	It is also specified that the numbers in the list must be less than 10.
each _+2	Additionally, it is specified that each number in the list is equal to the previous number plus 2.

In another example, the following formula can be used to create a list, including factorial values of number 1 to 5:

```
= List.Generate(()=> 1, each _<6, each _+1, each Number.
Factorial(_))
```

The inputs of this function are as shown in Table 6-5.

Table 6-5. *Parameters of List.Generate*

()=> 1,	The desired variable starts from 1.
each _<6,	The list continues until the variable is less than 6.
each _+1,	The value of the variable in each step is equal to its value in the previous step plus 1.
each Number. Factorial(_))	The factorial value of each variable should be displayed in the output.

According to the function explanation, the value of this formula is equal to {1,2,6,24,120}, where the first value is equal to factorial 1 and the third value is equal to factorial 3.

In another example, the result of the following formula is {2,4,8,16,32,64,128,256,512}:

```
= List.Generate(()=> 2, each _<1000, each _*2)
```

The inputs of this formula are as shown in Table 6-6.

Table 6-6. *Parameters of List.Generate*

()=> 2,	The variable starts from 2.
each _<1000,	The process is repeated until the variables are less than 1000.
each _*2	In each step, the value of the variable is equal to its previous value multiplied by 2.

According to the above explanation, the value of this formula is equal to a series of numbers where in each step, the desired number is obtained by multiplying the previous number by 2, and this process is repeated until the numbers are less than 1000. Therefore, the result is equal to {2,4,8,16,32,64,128,256,512}.

Another example of using List.Generate is presented in the following formula. This formula is used to create a list of numbers less than 10 in the Fibonacci sequence by using two variables, x, and y. (The Fibonacci sequence, which is {0, 1, 1, 2, 3, 5, 8, 13, ...}, is a sequence of numbers in which each number is the sum of the two previous numbers.)

```
= List.Generate(() => [x = 0, y = 1], each [x] < 10, each [x =
[y], y = [x]+[y]], each [x])
```

The different inputs of this function are as shown in Table 6-7.

Table 6-7. *Parameters of List.Generate*

`() => [x = 0, y = 1],`	Initially, the values of variables x and y are 0 and 1, respectively.
`each [x] < 10,`	The process of creating numbers in the list continues until variable x reaches a number greater than or equal to 10.
`each [x = [y], y = [x]+[y]],`	At each stage, the value of x is equal to the value of y in the previous stage, and the value of y is equal to the sum of the x and y values in the previous stage.
`each [x]`	Finally, the values for the x variable is shown in the output

According to the function explanation, the result of the formula is equal to {0,1,1,2,3,5,8}.

In the previous example, using each `[y]` instead of each `[x]` in the fourth argument means that the value of variable y is displayed in the output and the result is changed to {1,1,2,3,5,8,13}, and replacing the fourth argument by each `[x]+[y]` means that the sum of variables x and y will be displayed in the output, so the result will be {1,2,3,5,8,13,21}.

List.Times

`List.Times` is used as follows to create a list consisting of values in the format of time:

```
List.Times(
        start as time,
        count as number,
```

step as duration
) as list

This function takes three inputs as follows:

1. The first input is in time format and represents the first value of the list. Typically, the #time function is used to create this input.

2. The second input is in the number format and specifies the length of output list.

3. The third input is in duration format and specifies the difference between each time and its previous time in the list. Since the values in the desired list are in the format of time, their difference should be in the type of duration. Therefore, the #duration function is usually used to create this input.

Based on the function explanations, the result of the following formula is a list of {#time(1,10,0), #time(2,20,0), #time(3,30,0), #time(4,40,0)}:

List.Times(#time(1,10,0),4,#duration(0,1,10,0)).

List.Dates

This function is used as follows to create a list including values in the format of date:

List.Dates(
        start as date,
        count as number,
        step as duration
) as list

This function takes three arguments as follows:

1. The first argument specifies the initial data of the list and is usually defined using the #date() function.

2. The second input specifies the number of data that the list will contain.

3. The third input, which is considered as the step in the list, specifies the difference between each data and its previous data in the list. Since the data in the list are of type date, their difference should be of type duration and is usually defined using the #duration() function.

Based on the above explanation, the result of the following formula is equal to these three dates:

```
{#date(2021, 1, 12), #date(2021, 1, 13), #date(2021, 1, 14)}
List.Dates(#date(2021, 1, 12), 3, #duration(1, 0, 0, 0))
```

List.DateTimes

Like the List.Times and List.Date functions, which are used to create a list of values in the format of time or date, the List.DateTimes function is also used to create a list, but the output list contains both date and time values at the same time. This function can be defined as follows:

```
List.DateTimes(
start as datetime,
count as number,
step as duration
        ) as list
```

This function takes three inputs as follows:

1. In the first input, you specify the initial data and time of the desired list. Since the output list of this function contains values of type date and time, the #datetime() function is usually used in the first input of this function.

2. The number of members in the output list is specified in the second input of this function.

3. In the third input, which is known as the step, the difference between each value in the final list and its previous value is specified. The data entered in this input must be in the format of duration and is usually created using the #duration() function.

Based on the function explanations, the result of the following formula is equal to three dates and times:

```
{#datetime(2021, 1, 12,1,0,0), #datetime(2021, 1, 13,3,0,0),
#datetime(2021, 1, 14,5,0,0)}
List.Dates(#datetime(2021, 1, 12,1,0,0), 3, #duration(1,
2, 0, 0))
```

List.Random

List.Random is used as follows to create a list including random numbers between 0 and 1:

```
List.Random(
        count as number,
        optional seed as nullable number
            ) as list
```

This function takes two arguments as follows:

1. In the first argument, the length of the list is determining by entering an integer number.

2. The second argument is optional and represents the seed related to the generation of random numbers.

Based on the function explanation, the result of the formula List.Random(3) is equal to a list containing three random numbers in the range of 0 to 1.

Sorting Values in a List

As explained, lists in Power Query contain a set of values with a specific order. To change the order of values within a list, List.Reverse and List.Sort can be used.

List.Reverse

List.Reverse is very simple in Power Query and can be used to reverse the order of values in a list. This function takes an argument in the format of list, and displays the reversed list in the output as follows:

List.Reverse (**list** as list) as list

To clarify the use of this function, some examples of this function are provided in Table 6-8.

Table 6-8. *Examples for List.Reverse*

Formula	Result
= List.Reverse({1..4})	{4,3,2,1}
= List.Reverse({"a",1,"b",10})	{10,"b",1,"a"}
= List.Reverse({3,8,1})	{1,8,3}

List.Sort

By using List.Sort, values within a list can be sorted in ascending and descending, alphabetically, numerically, or any other logic. This function is defined as follows:

```
List.Sort(
    list as list,
    optional comparisonCriteria as any
        ) as list
```

Therefore, this function takes the following two arguments:

1. The reference list is defined in the first argument.

2. In the second argument of this function, the logic of sorting is specified. This input is optional; if not entered, the values in the list will be sorted in ascending order. However, Order.Descending can be entered in this input to sort the values in descending order. In advanced cases, the custom sorting logic can be defined by functions.

Some basic examples of this function are given in Table 6-9.

Table 6-9. Examples for List.Sort

Formula	Result
=List.Sort({1,5,-2,-3})	{-3,-2,1,5}
= List.Sort({1,5,2,3},Order.Descending)	{5,3,2,1}
= List.Sort({"a","x","b","c"})	{"a","b","c","x"}
= List.Sort({"a","x","b","c"},Order.Descending)	{"x","c","b","a"}

As shown in the previous examples, the result of the following formula is equal to {-3, -2, 1, 5}:

```
= List.Sort({1, 5, -2, -3})
```

This is because -3 is smaller than 1 and is listed at the beginning. But to compare the numbers without considering their signs, the following formula can be used:

```
= List.Sort({1, 5, -2, -3}, (x) => Number.Abs(x))
```

In this formula, you sort the values in the list by considering their absolute values instead of their original values. Therefore, the result of the above formula is equal to {1, -2, -3, 5}.

The following formulas can also used to sort the list without considering the value's signs from larger to smaller:

```
= List.Sort({1, 5, -2, -3}, {(x) => Number.Abs(x),Order.
Descending})
= List.Sort({1, 5, -2, -3}, {(x) => Number.Abs(x),1})
= List.Sort({1, 5, -2, -3}, {each Number.Abs(_),1})
```

In another example, by using the following formula, the even values are listed first in the output, followed by the odd values:

```
= List.Sort({1, 2, 5, 4, 3}, (x) => Number.IsOdd(x))
```

The output of the above formula is equal to {4, 2, 3, 1, 5}, in which all even values come first and are followed by odd values. To sort odd and even values in their groups from smallest to the largest, the following formula can be used:

```
= List.Sort({1, 2, 5, 4, 3}, {{each Number.IsOdd(_)},{each _}})
```

Two-step sorting is defined in the above formula. Initially, values are sorted based on {each Number.IsOdd(_)}. Then, if the result of this formula is equal for several values, they get sorted based on the {each _} criteria (from smaller to larger). So, the result is {2,4,1,3,5}

In another example, instead of considering the first character (left character) for sorting the texts into a list, the last character (right character) is used as the basis for sorting in the next formula:

```
= List.Sort({"AXY", "XYA", "WND", "ACC"}, each Text.End(_, 1))
```

The result of the above formula is equal to {"XYA", "ACC", "WND", "AXY"}.

Extracting from a List

In Power Query, there are many functions for extracting values from a list, which are examined in this section.

List.First and List.Last

List.First is used to extract the value in a list and List.Last is used to extract the last value in the list as follows:

```
List.First(
list as list,
optional defaultValue as any
) as any
```

```
List.Last(
        list as list,
        optional defaultValue as any
            ) as any
```

Both functions take the following arguments:

1. The reference list is entered in the first argument.

2. The second argument of these functions is optional, and it is shown in the output if the reference list is empty.

Based on the function explanation, the result of the following formula is equal to 1:

```
= List.First({1..10})
```

And the result of the following formula is equal to -1:

```
= List.First({ },-1)
```

List.FirstN and List.LastN

These functions are like each other, with the difference that `List.FirstN` is used to extract a specific number of values from the beginning of the list, and `List.LastN` is used to extract a specific number of values from the end of the list. Both are defined as follows:

```
List.FirstN)
        list as list,
        countOrCondition as any
            ) as any
```

```
List.LastN(
        list as list,
        optional countOrCondition as any
            ) as any
```

These functions take two inputs, where the first input is in a list format and the second input is in a numerical format.

1. A reference list is entered in the first input.

2. In this input, the number of values to extract from the beginning (or end) of the list is entered. In this input, the filtering condition can also be defined instead of a specific number. In this case, the largest set of values from the beginning (or end) of the list that meets the relevant condition is displayed as the output. In other words, the values from the beginning (or end) of the list are extracted until the first example of a noncompliance is observed.

Based on the function explanation, the output of these functions in different examples is given in Table 6-10.

Table 6-10. *Examples for List.FirstN*

Formula	Result
= List.FirstN({1..10},3)	{1,2,3}
= List.FirstN({1..10},5)	{1,2,3,4,5}
= List.FirstN({1..10},each _<5)	{1,2,3,4}
= List.FirstN({5, 4,1, 2, 6, 1}, each _>3)	{5.4}
= List.LastN({1..10},3)	{8,9,10}
= List.LastN({1..10},5)	{6,7,8,9,10}
= List.LastN({1..10},each _<5)	{1,2,3,4}
= List.LastN({5, 4,1, 2, 6, 1}, each _<3)	{1}

In the example of List.LastN({5, 4,1, 2, 6, 1}, each _<3), it is expressed that the values at the end of the list that are smaller than 3 should be displayed in the output. As you can see, the reference list also includes the number 2 (which is smaller than 3 and meets the condition),

117

but the output only includes the number 1. The reason is that the values at the end of the list are displayed in the output if the condition is met, and as soon as a value that does not meet the condition is encountered, the search operation stops, and the next values are not examined. Therefore, in this example, since the number 6 (the second to last data) is greater than 3, the data before the number 6 are not examined.

List.Range

This function is used to extract values from different parts of a list and is defined as follows:

```
List.Range(
        list as list,
        offset as number,
        optional count as nullable number
            ) as list
```

This function takes the following three inputs:

1. In the first input of this function, the reference list is entered.

2. In this input, the starting point for extracting values is determined by entering a number.

3. The third input of this function indicates the number of values for extracting from the list.

Different examples of this function are listed in Table 6-11.

Table 6-11. *Examples for List.Range*

Formula	Result
= List.Range({1..10},5,3)	{6,7,8}
= List.Range({1..10},1,3)	{2,3,4}
= List.Range({1..10},3,1)	{4}

List.Max and List.Min

List.Max and List.Min are used to extract the largest and smallest value in a list as follows:

```
List.Max(
    list as list,
    optional default as any,
    optional comparisonCriteria as any,
    optional includeNulls as nullable logical
        ) as any

List.Min(
    list as list,
    optional default as any,
    optional comparisonCriteria as any,
    optional includeNulls as nullable logical
        ) as any
```

These functions take the following four inputs, where only the first input is mandatory and the others are optional:

1. The reference list is entered in the first input.

2. The second input is optional and specifies the result of the function if it is equal to null (the reference list is empty).

3. The third input of this function, which is also optional, specifies the criterion for comparing values.

4. The fourth input of this function can be True (for considering Null values) or False (for neglecting Null values).

Based on the function explanation, the result of these functions for different examples is provided in Table 6-12.

Table 6-12. *Examples for List.Max*

Formula	Result
=List.Max({1..10})	10
= List.Max({},-1)	-1
= List.Max({"a".."n"},-1)	"n"
= List.Max({-20..10},null,each Number.Abs(_))	-20

List.MaxN and List.MinN

List.MaxN and List.MinN are used to extract the n largest or smallest values within a list as follows:

```
List.MinN(
      list as list,
      countOrCondition as any,
      optional comparisonCriteria as any,
      optional includeNulls as nullable logical
            ) as list
```

```
List.MaxN(
        list as list,
        countOrCondition as any,
        optional comparisonCriteria as any,
        optional includeNulls as nullable logical
        ) as list
```

According to the above syntax, these functions take these four inputs:

1. A reference list is entered in the first input.

2. In the second input of these functions, the number n (the number of largest or smallest values for extracting) or the condition for extracting is determined.

3. The third input of this function, which is optional, expresses the logic of comparing the data.

4. The fourth input is optional and can be one of the values True (for considering Null values) or False (for neglecting Null values).

Based on the function explanation, the results of different states of these functions are listed in Table 6-13.

Table 6-13. *Examples for List.MaxN*

Formula	Result
= List.MaxN({-20..10},3)	{10,9,8}
= List.MaxN({"a",1,-1,"N"},3)	{"a","N",1}

List.Select

`List.Select` is one of the most important and powerful functions in Power Query for extracting the values from a list based on the custom condition by the following syntax:

```
List.Select(
    list as list,
    selection as function
        ) as list
```

This function takes two inputs, and its output is always a list.

1. The first input is the reference list.

2. The second input defines the condition for selecting values from the reference list as a function. Various scenarios can be defined for this input, which are discussed below.

Let's start with an example. In the formula `List.Select({1..10}, each _>5)`, the reference list is a list of numbers from 1 to 10 and the condition is defined as `each _>5`, meaning that numbers greater than 5 in the reference list should be extracted and displayed in the output. Therefore, the result of this formula is equal to the list {6,7,8,9,10}.

Different examples of this function are provided in Table 6-14.

Table 6-14. *Examples for List.Select*

Function	Result
= List.Select({1..10},each _>5)	{6,7,8,9,10}
= List.Select({1..10},each _>5 and _<8)	{6,7}
= List.Select({1..10},each Number.IsOdd(_))	{1,3,5,7,9}
= List.Select({1..10},each Number.Mod(_,3)=0)	{3,6,9}
= List.Select({1,"a",3,"x","n"},each Value. Is(_,type number))	{1,3}

In the previous examples, the condition each Number.IsOdd(_) means that only odd values should be extracted from the reference list, and the condition each Number.Mod(_,3)=0 means that only numbers that are multiples of 3 should be extracted from the list, and finally, the condition each Value.Is(_,type number) means that only values of type number should be extracted from the reference list.

List.FindText

To extract text values from a list that contains one specific character or text, List.FindText with the following syntax can be used:

```
List.FindText(
        list as list,
        text as text
            ) as list
```

This function contains these two inputs:

1. The reference list is entered in the first input.

2. The text that you want to search for is entered in this input. For example, entering "a" in this input means that values from the reference list containing the letter "a" will be displayed in the output, and entering "ab" means that values from the reference list containing the letters "ab" will be displayed as the output.

Based on the function explanation, some examples of the application of this function are provided in Table 6-15.

Table 6-15. *Examples for List.FindText*

Formula	Result
=List.FindText({"a".."z"},"m")	{"m"}
= List.FindText({"a".."z"},"M")	{}
= List.FindText({"abc","bcf","deg","z"},"b")	{"Abc","bcf"}

Removing Values in a List

In Power Query, there are many functions for removing values from a list, which are examined in this section.

List.RemoveNull

This function is used to remove null values from a list by the following syntax:

```
List.RemoveNulls(list as list) as list
```

This function takes only one input in the form of list, and after removing null values in that list, the result will display in the output.

According to the above explanation, the result of the following formula is equal to {1,2,"",3,"null"}:

```
= List.RemoveNulls({1,null,2,null,"",3,"null"})
```

As you can see, the output of this formula also includes the value "null" because the word null is entered in double quotes and considered as a text value and this function does not consider this value as null.

List.Distinct

List.Distinct is used to remove duplicate values in a list and always results in a list with unique values.

```
List.Distinct(
    list as list,
    optional equationCriteria as any
    ) as list
```

The function takes two arguments as follows:

1. The reference list is entered in the first argument.

2. The second argument of this function is optional and allows you to specify custom criteria for comparing the values.

Based on the above explanation, the result of this function for different examples is shown in Table 6-16.

Table 6-16. *Examples for List.Distinct*

Formula	Result
= List.Distinct({1,3,2,1,2,5,1})	{1,3,2,5}
= List.Distinct({1,1,1,1,1,1,1})	{1}
= List.Distinct({"a","A","b","a"})	{"a","A","b"}
= List.Distinct({"a","A","b","a"},Comparer. OrdinalIgnoreCase)	{"a","b"}
= List.Distinct({1..10},each Number.IsOdd(_))	{1,2}

List.RemoveFirsN and List.RemoveLastN

List.RemoveFirsN and List.RemoveLastN are used to remove a specific number of values from the beginning or ending of a list, as follows:

```
List.RemoveFirstN(
        list as list,
        optional countOrCondition as any
            ) as list
```

```
List.RemoveLastN(
        list as list,
        optional countOrCondition as any
            ) as list
```

These functions take two arguments as follows:

1. A reference list is entered in the first argument.

2. The second input determines how many values should be removed from the beginning or end of the reference list.

List.RemoveRange

List.RemoveRange is used to remove values in a list by the following syntax:

```
List.RemoveRange(
    list as list,
    index as number,
    optional count as nullable number
) as list
```

This function takes three inputs as follows:

1. A reference list is entered in the first input.

2. In this input, the starting point for removing the values is determined.

3. The third input determines how many values should be removed from the starting point (determined in the second input) in the reference list.

Multiple examples of using List.RemoveRange are provided in Table 6-17.

Table 6-17. *Examples for List.RemoveRange*

Formula	Result
= List.RemoveRange({1..10},3,5)	{1,2,3,9}
= List.RemoveRange({1..10},4,4)	{1,2,3,4,9,10}

List.RemoveItems

Using `List.RemoveItems` with the following syntax, specific values can be removed from a list:

```
List.RemoveItems(
        list1 as list,
        list2 as list
            ) as list
```

This function takes the following two inputs in the format of a list:

1. The first input is the reference list.

2. The second input of this function is a list of values that you want to remove from the reference list.

Based on the provided explanation, in the formula below, the reference list includes all numbers from 1 to 10. The second input states that numbers 3 to 8 should be removed from the reference list. Therefore, the result of this formula is equal to {1,2,9,10}:

```
=List.RemoveItems({1..10},{3..8})
```

Additionally, the `List.RemoveMatchingItems` function is used to remove values from a reference list; the difference is that this function receives three inputs, and the matching criterion can be determined in the third input.

```
List.RemoveMatchingItems(
        list1 as list,
        list2 as list,
        optional equationCriteria as any
            ) as list
```

List.Skip

List.Skip is like List.RemoveFirstN and is used to remove a number of values or values with specific conditions from the beginning of a list, as follows:

```
List.Skip(
    list as list,
    optional countOrCondition as any
        ) as list
```

This function receives these two inputs:

1. In the first input of this function, the reference list is entered.

2. In the second input, the number of values for removing from the beginning of the list or the removing condition is entered.

According to the function explanation, the result of the following formula is equal to {5,6,7}:

```
=List.Skip({1..7},4)
```

Similarly, the result of the following formula is also equal to {5,6,7}:

```
= List.Skip({1..7},each _<5)
```

List.Alternate

List.Alternate with the following syntax is used to remove and retain a series of values in a list with a specific pattern (e.g., removing every other values):

```
List.Alternate(
    list as list,
    count as number,
```

```
    optional repeatInterval as nullable number,
    optional offset as nullable number
        ) as list
```

This function takes these four inputs:

1. The reference list is entered in the first input.

2. In the second input, the number of values for skipping in each iteration is determined.

3. The third input determines how many values are selected between the skipped values.

4. This input is optional and determines the starting point for skipping values. Entering the number 2 in this input means the first two values of the list should be retained (displayed in the output) and the pattern of skipping and retaining values starts from the third value in the list.

According to the above explanation, the following formula specifies that only the first value in the reference list should be removed and the other values should report in the result. Therefore, the result of this formula is equal to {2..10}.

```
= List.Alternate({1..10}, 1)
```

In the following formula, it is specified that every other value should be skipped in the list. Therefore, the result of the formula is equal to all even values in the list and is equal to {2,4,6,8,10}.

```
= List.Alternate({1..10}, 1,1)
```

In the following formula, it is specified that in each iteration, one value should be skipped and the next two values should remain, and this process continues until the end of the list. Therefore, the result of the formula is {2,3,5,6,8,9}.

```
= List.Alternate({1..10}, 1,2)
```

And the following example is the opposite of the previous example, where in each iteration, two values are skipped and the next value remains. Therefore, the result of the following formula is equal to {3,6,9}:

```
= List.Alternate({1..10}, 2,1)
```

The following formula is like the above formula, with the difference that the pattern is executed after the second value in the list. {1,2,5,8}

```
= List.Alternate({1..10}, 2,1,2)
```

List Merging

There are multiple functions in Power Query for merging two or more lists together and they are explained in this section. In addition to the existing functions, lists can be merged easily by using the & operator. So {1,2} & {1,4,3} is {1,2,1,4,3}. However, to examine more advanced list merging scenarios, the following functions should be used.

List.Combine

This function is used to merge two or more lists together as follows:

```
List.Combine(lists as list) as list
```

This function takes one input, in the format of list, so all the lists (that you want to combine) must be placed inside a reference list as the input of this function. Then, in the output of this function, all the lists provided inside that reference list are merged and displayed in a new list.

So the result of the following formula is equal to {1,2,1,4,3}:

```
= List.Combine({{1,2},{1,4,3}})
```

And the result of the following formula is equal to {1,2,1,3,1,3}:

```
= List.Combine({ {1,2},{1,3},{1,3}})
```

List.InsertRange

To add new values (a list of values) to a list in a specific position, `List.InsertRange` can be used as follows:

```
List.InsertRange(
        list as list,
        index as number,
        values as list
              ) as list
```

This function takes these three inputs:

1. The first input represents the reference list.

2. In the second input of this function, the position of adding new values is determined by entering a number.

3. The values that you want to add to the reference list are inserted in a list in this input.

Based on the function explanation, the result of this function in different formulas is shown in Table 6-18.

Table 6-18. *Examples for List.InsertRange*

Formula	Result
= List.InsertRange({"abc","bcf", "deg","z"},2,{"b","a"})	{"abc","bcf", b","a","deg","z" }
= List.InsertRange({1..5},2,{1..3})	{1,2,1,2,3,3,4,5}
= List.InsertRange({1..5},1,{1..3})	{1,1,2,3,1,3,4,5}

List.Zip

To combine the corresponding values of several lists, List.Zip can be used as follows:

List.Zip(**lists** as list) as list

This function receives an input in the form of a list. The entered list includes several lists and their corresponding values come to gather in separate list in the output.

For example, entering {{1..3},{4..5}} in the first input of this function results in {{1,4},{2,5},{3,null}}.

In a similar case, the result of the formula = List.Zip({{1..4}, {3..5},{2..7}}) is equal to the following list:

={1,3,2},{2,4,3},{3,5,4},{4,null,5},{null,null,6},
{null,null,7}}

List.Union

List.Union with the following syntax is used to combine two or more lists, like the List.Combine function. The difference is that this function neglects duplicate values (values repeated in all lists).

```
List.Union(
     lists as list,
     optional equationCriteria as any
          ) as list
```

This function receives the two following inputs:

1. The first input of this function is the reference list, which includes the lists you want to merge.

2. The second input of this function allows you to specify custom criteria for comparing the values.

Therefore, the result of this function is as shown in Table 6-19 for different examples.

Table 6-19. *Examples for List.Union*

Formula	Result
= List.Union({{1,2},{1,4,3}})	{1,2,4,3}
= List.Union({{1,2,1},{1,4,3}})	{1,2,1,4,3}
= List.Union({{1,2},{1,3},{1,3}})	{1,2,3}
= List.Union({{1,2,3,2},{1,3,2,4}})	{1,2,3,2,4}
= List.Union({{1,2},{1,3},{1,4,1}})	{1,2,1,3,4}

List.Intersect

List.Intersect with the following syntax is used to extract common values in two or more lists:

```
List.Intersect(
     lists as list,
     optional equationCriteria as any
          ) as list
```

134

The output includes values that have been repeated in all the input lists. This function takes two arguments.

1. The first argument indicates a reference list containing a set of lists for which that you want to calculate the intersection.

2. The second argument is used to specify custom criteria for comparing the elements in the lists.

According to the function explanation, the result of this function for different cases is as shown in Table 6-20.

Table 6-20. *Examples for List.Intersect*

Formula	Result
= List.Intersect({{1..4},{2..5}})	{2,3,4}
= List.Intersect({{1..4},{2..5},{3..6}})	{3,4}
= List.Intersect({{1,2},{1,3},{1,4,1}})	{1}

List.Difference

List.Difference is used to calculate the difference between two lists and always results in a list of values that exists in the first list but not in the second list.

```
List.Difference(
     list1 as list,
     list2 as list,
     optional equationCriteria as any
          ) as list
```

The function takes three inputs as follows:

1. The first list is inserted in the first input.

2. The second list is inserted in the second input.

3. This optional input allows the user to specify custom criteria for comparing the values.

Based on this explanation, the result of this function for different input cases is as shown in Table 6-21.

Table 6-21. *Examples for List.Difference*

Formula	Result
= List.Difference({1..10},{3..12})	{1,2}
= List.Difference({3..12},{1..10})	{11,12}
= List.Difference({3..12},{1..30})	{}

Mathematical Calculations on the Data of a List

There are several functions in Power Query that receive a list as input and, after performing mathematical operations on the values of the list, display a value (number) as output. One of the most famous of these functions is List.Count, which can be used to extract the length of a list. So, the result of the following formula is equal to the count of numbers in the list, equal to 5:

=List.Count({1..5})

There are other functions that are divided into the following groups. Functions in the first group are listed in Table 6-22 and all receive a list as input.

Table 6-22. *Application of Mathematic Functions on Lists*

Function	Result
List.Count	Number of values in the reference list
List.NonNullCount	Number of non-null values in the reference list
List.StandardDeviation	The standard deviation of the values in the reference list

The second group includes the functions listed in Table 6-23.

Table 6-23. *Application of Mathematical Functions on Lists*

Function	Result
List.Sum	Calculates the total of all numbers in the list
List.Product	Calculates the product of all numbers in the reference list
List.Average	Calculates the average of all numbers in the list

These functions receive two inputs.

1. The reference list is entered in the first input.

2. The precision of calculations (optional), which can be either Precision.Double or Precision.Decimal, is entered in the second input.

The next group includes List.Mode and List.Median to calculate the mode and median of numbers in the list. They are defined as follows:

```
List.Median(
    list as list,
    optional comparisonCriteria as any
        ) as any
```

137

```
List.Mode(
    list as list,
    optional equationCriteria as any
        ) as any
```

These functions receive two inputs as follows:

1. The reference list is entered in the first input.

2. This input allows you to specify custom criteria for comparing the values.

List.Percentile is another function in this group, which is used to extract the nth percentile as follows:

```
List.Percentile(
    list as list,
    percentiles as any,
    optional options as nullable record
        ) as any
```

This function receives three inputs in this order: the reference list, the desired percentile (which is entered as a decimal number such as 0.25), and precision.

Based on the above explanation, Table 6-24 provides multiple examples of the results of this function.

Table 6-24. *Examples for Mathematical Functions on Lists*

Formula	Result
List.Count({1..10,4})	10
List.NonNullCount({1..10,4})	10
List.StandardDeviation({1..10,4})	2.788867
List.Sum({1..10,4})	50
List.Product({1..10,4})	1612800
List.Average({1..10,4})	5
List.Mode({1..10,4})	4
List.Median.({1..10,4})	4.5
List.Percentile({1..10,4},0.25)	3.25

List Information Functions

To check the equality of two lists, the = operator can be used between the two lists, like the following formula:

={1,2,3}={1,3,2}

In checking the equality of two lists, the result will be True only if the values in the both list are same (in terms of value and format) and also in the same order. Since in the above formula, the numbers 3 and 2 in the second list have been swapped compared to the first list, the result of the above formula will be False, but the result of the following formula will be True:

={1,2,3}={1,2,3}

Besides the check equality of two lists, to check the existence of value(s) in a list, several functions can be used in Power Query, and the result of these functions will be True or False based on the condition.

In the following formulas, checking the existence of a value within the list under consideration is discussed.

List.IsEmpty

To check a list is empty or includes at least a value, `List.IsEmpty` can be used as below:

```
List.IsEmpty(list as list) as logical
```

This function receives a list as input, and if at least one value is registered inside the input list, the result of this formula is False, and if the list does not contain any value, the result of this function is True.

In other words, in the following state, the result of this function is True, and in other cases, the result of this function is False:

```
=List.Empthy({ })
```

List.IsDistinct

To check for duplicate values within a list, the List.IsDistinct function can be used as follows:

```
List.IsDistinct(
        list as list,
        optional equationCriteria as any
            ) as logical
```

According to the function syntax, this function receives these two inputs:

1. In the first input, the reference list is entered.

2. The second input of this function (which is optional) allows you to specify custom criteria for comparing the values in the list. If not entered, sensitivity to uppercase and lowercase letters is shown in text comparisons.

If the reference list contains duplicate values based on the logic defined in the second input, the result of this function is False; otherwise, the result of this function is True.

Based on the function explanation, the result of the following formula is True:

```
= List.IsDistinct({1..10})
```

And the result of the following formula is False.

```
= List.IsDistinct({1..10,1})
```

List.Contains

Using List.Contains, the existence of a specific value (just one value) in a reference list can be checked. This function is defined as follows:

```
List.Contains(
        list as list,
        value as any,
        optional equationCriteria as any
              ) as logical
```

According to the above syntax, this function takes three inputs:

1. The reference list is entered in the first input.

2. In the second input of this function, the value that you want to check for existence in the reference list is entered.

3. The third input of this function is optional and allows you to specify custom criteria for comparing the values.

The output of this function is True if the reference list contains the value registered in the second input and False in other cases. Therefore, the result of the following formula is True:

```
= List.Contains({1..10},3)
```

And the result of the following formula is False:

```
= List.Contains({1..10},11)
```

List.ContainsAll

To check the existence of two or more values within a list, `List.ContainsAll` can be used as follows:

```
List.ContainsAll(
        list as list,
        values as list,
        optional equationCriteria as any
                ) as logical
```

This function takes these three inputs:

1. The reference is entered in the first input.

2. The list of values that you want to check for their existence in the reference list is entered in the second input.

3. The third input allows you to specify custom criteria for comparing the values.

The result of this function is True if the reference list contains all the values in the second input; in other cases, the result of this function is False.

Some simple examples of this function are provided in Table 6-25.

Table 6-25. *Examples for List.ContainsAll*

Formula	Result
= List.ContainsAll({1..10},{1,3,7})	True
= List.ContainsAll({1..10},{1,3,11})	False

List.ContainsAny

List.ContainsAny is like List.ContainsAll, with the difference that the result of List.ContainsAny is true if the reference list contains at least one value in the second input.

The List.ContainsAny is defined as follows:

```
List.ContainsAny(
    list as list,
    values as list,
    optional equationCriteria as any
        ) as logical
```

This function takes three inputs.

1. The reference list is entered in the first input.

2. The list of values to check for their existence in the reference list is entered in the second input.

3. The logic to compare the values is defined in the third input and allows you to specify custom criteria for comparing the values.

Some simple examples of this function are provided in Table 6-26.

143

Table 6-26. *Examples for List.ContainsAny*

Formula	Result
= List.ContainsAny({1..10},{1,3,7})	True
= List.ContainsAny({1..10},{1,3,11})	True
= List.ContainsAny({1..10},{12,13,11})	False

List.AllTrue

This function receives a list as input, and if all the values in the reference list are equal to True, the result of this function is True; otherwise, the result of this function is False. It is defined as follows:

```
List.AllTrue(list as list) as logical
```

It should be noted that the list entered in this function must contain True or False values, and if it includes a number or text, the result of this function is an error.

List.AnyTrue

This function is defined as follows:

```
List.AnyTrue(list as list) as logical
```

This function receives a list as input, and if at least one of the values in that list is equal to True, the result of this function is True; otherwise, the result of this function is False.

Positions in a List

The functions related to extracting the position of values in a list are explained in this section.

List.Positions

The List.Positions function is defined very simply in Power Query as follows:

```
List.Positions(list as list) as list
```

This function takes a list as input and its output is equal to a list explaining the position of values. The output of this function is only dependent on the number of values in the reference list and is not dependent on their value or type. In other words, the result of this function is always equal to {0,1} for lists with two values and {0,1,2} for lists with three values.

Therefore, the result of the following formula is equal to {0,1,2}:

```
=List.Positions({1,10,-1})
```

List.PositionOf

To extract the position of a value, List.PositionOf can be used as follows:

```
List.PositionOf(
        list as list,
        value as any,
        optional occurrence as nullable number,
        optional equationCriteria as any
            ) as any
```

This function takes four inputs.

1. The first input is the reference list.

2. The value of the position you are searching for is entered in the second input.

3. The third input is optional, and it is used if the searching value has been repeated more than once in the reference list. This input specifies which repetition presents in the output. Entering Occurrence.First means the position of the first repetition is displayed in the output. Using Occurrence.Last means the position of the last repetition is displayed. Finally, by using the Occurrence.All, the positions of all repetitions are displayed in the output as a list.

4. The fourth input of this function is also optional and allows you to specify custom criteria for comparing the values.

Various examples of this function are given in Table 6-27.

Table 6-27. *Examples for List.PositionOf*

Formula	Result
= List.PositionOf({1..10},5)	4
= List.PositionOf({4,5,3,5,2},5)	1
= List.PositionOf({4,5,3,5,2},5,Occurrence.First)	1
= List.PositionOf({4,5,3,5,2},5,Occurrence.Last)	3
= List.PositionOf({4,5,3,5,2},5,Occurrence.All)	{1,3}
= List.PositionOf({"a","b","A","A"},"A")	2

List.PositionOfAny

`List.PositionOfAny` is like `List.Position`, but with the difference that in this function, it is possible to search for two or more values simultaneously within a reference list and extract their positions. This function is defined as follows:

```
List.PositionOfAny(
        list as list,
        values as list,
        optional occurrence as nullable number,
        optional equationCriteria as any
            ) as any
```

`List.PositionOfAny` takes four inputs.

1. In the first input, the reference list is entered.

2. In the second input, the list of values for the positions you are searching for is entered.

3. The third input of this function is optional and is used if the searching values are repeated in the reference list several times. In this input, entering `Occurrence.First` means the first repetition is presented by the function, and entering `Occurrence.Last` means the last repetition is presented. To determine all repetitions, Occurrence. All can be used in this function.

4. The fourth input of this function is optional and allows you to specify custom criteria for comparing the values.

Various examples of this function are provided in Table 6-28.

Table 6-28. *Examples for List.PositonOfAny*

Formula	Result
= List.PositionOfAny({1..10},5)	4
= List.PositionOfAny({4,5,3,5,2},5)	1
= List.PositionOfAny({4,5,3,5,2},{5,3},Occurrence. First)	1
= List.PositionOfAny({4,5,3,5,2},{3},Occurrence.Last)	3
= List.PositionOfAny({4,5,3,5,2},{5,3},Occurrence.All)	{1,2,3}
= List.PositionOfAny({"a","b","A","A"},{"a","A"})	0

Replacing and Transforming Values

There are functions in Power Query that allow you to replace the values in a list with new values.

List.ReplaceValue

Using List.ReplaceValue means a value in a list can be replaced with a new value as follows:

```
List.ReplaceValue(
        list as list,
        oldValue as any,
        newValue as any,
        replacer as function
            ) as list
```

This function takes four inputs.

1. The reference list is entered in the first input.

2. The second input represents the old value that you want to replace with a new value.

3. The new value is entered in the third input.

4. The fourth input of this function represents the type of replacement, which is defined as a function. In this input, two modes, Replacer.ReplaceValue and Replacer.ReplaceText, can be used to replace numbers and text, respectively.

Based on the function explanation, the result of this function in different modes is shown in Table 6-29.

Table 6-29. *Examples for List.ReplaceValue*

Formula	Result
= List.ReplaceValue({1..4},4,3,Replacer. ReplaceValue)	{1,2,3,3}
= List.ReplaceValue({1..4},4,3,Replacer. ReplaceText)	{1,2,3,4}
= List.ReplaceValue({"a","b","B"},"b","B", Replacer.ReplaceText)	{"a","B","B"}

List.ReplaceMatchingItems

List.ReplaceMatchingItems is like List.ReplaceItems, but List. ReplaceItems can only replace one value of the list with a new value, whereas List.ReplaceMatchingItems can be used to replace multiple values of a list with new values. This function is defined as follows:

```
List.ReplaceMatchingItems(
     list as list,
     replacements as list,
     optional equationCriteria as any
          ) as list
```

This function takes three inputs.

1. The first input defines the reference list.

2. The second input is defined as a list of lists in which all internal lists include two values. The first presents the old value and the second presents the new value. So, to replace 1 with -1 and 4 with -4 in a list, this input is defined as {{1,-1},{4,-4}}.

3. The third input of this function is optional and allows you to specify custom criteria for comparing the values.

Based on the function explanation, the result of this function in different examples is shown in Table 6-30.

Table 6-30. *Examples for List.ReplaceMatchingItems*

Formula	Result
= List.ReplaceMatchingItems({1..5},{{1,5}})	{5,2,3,4,5}
= List.ReplaceMatchingItems({1..5},{{1,5},{2,6}})	{5,6,3,4,5}

List.ReplaceRange

To replace a part of a list based on its position (for example, from the 5th to the 12th values) by new values, List.ReplaceRange can be used as follows:

```
List.ReplaceRange(
        list as list,
        index as number,
        count as number,
        replaceWith as list
            ) as list
```

This function takes four inputs.

1. The first input represents the reference list.

2. In the second input of this function, the starting position for removing values from the list is specified. (The numbering starts from 0).

3. The number of values that should be removed is determined in the third input of this function.

4. In the fourth input, the list of values that should replace the deleted values is entered.

Based on the inputs of this function, multiple examples of this function are provided in Table 6-31.

Table 6-31. Examples for List.ReplaceRange

Formula	Result
= List.ReplaceRange({1..10},3,6,{5})	{1,2,3,5,10}
= List.ReplaceRange({1..10},0,6,{5})	{5,7,8,9,10}
= List.ReplaceRange({1..10},1,8,{5,6})	{1,5,6,10}

List.Transform

List.Transform can be used to change the values in a list by specific logic or operation. For example, with this function, all values can be added to the number 1, or multiplied by 2, English letters can be converted to uppercase or lowercase, or extra spaces can be removed. This function is defined as follows:

```
List.Transform(
    list as list,
    transform as function
        ) as list
```

This function receives two inputs.

1. The first input of this function defines the reference list.

2. The second input of this function is in the form of a function and determines the transforming logic.

There are different ways to define the second input, but in the simplest ones, you can enter the word each at the beginning of this input. Then the "_" determines the values in the list, so each _+2 can be used to add 2 in all the values in the list or each Number.Abs(_) can be used to remove the values sign.

In another way, instead of mentioning each and then using "_" for values in the list, a specific variable like x can be used in the parenthesis and then the operation is determined after =>. So (x) => x+1 can be used in the second input to add 1 to all values in the list.

With the above explanation, various examples of this function are provided in Table 6-32.

Table 6-32. *Examples for List.Transform*

Formula	Result
= List.Transform({1..5},each _+ 2)	{3,4,5,6,7}
= List.Transform({1..5},each Number.Factorial(_))	{1,2,6,24,120}
= List.Transform({1..5},each Number. Round(Number.Exp(_)))	{3,7,20,55,148}
= List.Transform({"abc","DEF","mNg"}, each Text.Proper(_))	{"Abc","Def","Mng"}

List.TransformMany

List.TransformMany can be used to change or transform values in a list by specific logic as follows:

```
List.TransformMany(
    list as list,
    collectionTransform as function,
    resultTransform as function
        ) as list
```

Based on this syntax, this function takes three inputs.

1. The first input defines the reference list.

2. In the second input, the transforming function is defined.

3. In the third input, the method of retransforming function is defined. In other words, by considering the first input as x, the function defined in the second input is in the form of (x) =>, and its result is considered as y. In the third input of this function, a new function is defined in the form of (x, y) =>.

In the following formula, the reference list (x) is {1,2,3}, and based on the function defined in the second input, the second list (y) is {2,4,6}. Considering these two lists, the result of the formula is {"1-2", "2-4", "3-6"}.

```
= List.TransformMany(
    {1,2,3},
    (x) => {2*x},
    (x,y) => (Text.From(x) & "-" & Text.From(y))
)
```

Other Functions

In addition to the above-mentioned functions, there are other functions in Power Query for modifying a list.

List.Single

This function receives an input in the form of a list. If the list has only one value, it displays that value as output. Otherwise, the result of this function is an error. This function is defined as follows:

```
List.Single(list as list) as any
```

Therefore, the result of the formula List.Single({1}) is the number 1, and the result of the formula List.Single({1..4}) is an error. Also, the result of the formula List.Single({ }) is null.

List.SingleOrDefault

This function is like the List.Single function, but in this function, it is possible to specify a value to be displayed in the output instead of an error. This function is defined in Power Query as follows:

```
List.SingleOrDefault(
        list as list,
        optional default as any
            ) as any
```

This function receives two inputs.

1.   The first input defines the reference list.

2.   The second input of this function is optional, and
     if the result of the function is an error, the value
     entered in this input is displayed instead of the error.

Therefore, the result of the formula `List.SingleOrDefault({1})`
is equal to the number 1, and the result of the formula `List.`
`SingleOrDefault({1..4})` is an error, but the result of the formula `List.`
`SingleOrDefault({1..4}, -1)` is equal to -1.

List.Repeat

Using `List.Repeat`, it is possible to repeat the values of a list in specific
numbers as follows:

```
List.Repeat(
        list as list,
        count as number
            ) as list
```

This function takes two inputs.

1.   The first input represents the reference list.

2.   The number of repetitions of values in the list is
     determined by this input.

Based on the function explanation, the result of this function is given in Table 6-33 under different conditions.

Table 6-33. *Examples for List.Repeat*

Formula	Result
=List.Repeat({1,2},2)	{1,2,1,2}
= List.Repeat({1..3},2)	{1,2,3,1,2,3}
= List.Repeat({1,2},3)	{1,2,1,2,1,2}

List.Split

By using this function with the following syntax, a large list can be converted into several smaller lists:

```
List.Split(
    list as list,
    pageSize as number
        ) as list
```

This function receives two inputs.

1. The first input defines the reference list.

2. The second input determines the length of the subset lists. For example, by entering 2 in this input, the reference list is divided into several lists with a length of 2.

Based on the function explanation, the result of this function is provided in several examples in Table 6-34.

Table 6-34. *Examples for List.Split*

Formula	Result
= List.Split({1..5},2)	{{1,2},{3,4},{5}}
= List.Split({1..5},3)	{{1,2,3},{4,5}}
= List.Split({1..5},4)	{{1,2,3,4},{5}}

Summary

In this chapter, you embarked on an exploration of the versatile and dynamic world of list functions within Power Query. Lists, as collections of data points, play a pivotal role in understanding data relationships and dependencies, and mastering their manipulation opens doors to intricate data transformations.

Your journey commenced by understanding the fundamental nature of lists, their ordered structure, and their ability to hold heterogeneous data types. You learned how to manually create lists and generate them dynamically through calculated expressions, establishing a foundation for advanced list manipulation.

As you delved deeper, you discovered the power of list functions that Power Query offers. These functions enable you to reshape data collections, from filtering and sorting elements to merging lists to create cohesive data structures. This versatility allows you to address complex data manipulation challenges with precision.

Furthermore, you explored the realm of nested lists, where lists within lists create hierarchies that mirror real-world relationships. This skill is invaluable when dealing with multidimensional data structures and navigating their complexities.

At the heart of your journey is the concept of aggregation and summarization. You uncovered the potential of list functions to distill extensive datasets into concise insights. Techniques for calculating totals, averages, and identifying trends empower you to extract meaningful information from the sea of data points.

In the next chapter, you will familiarize yourself with functions related to modifying records, including extracting specific values from records, merging lists, and modifying record properties.

CHAPTER 7

Records

In the symphony of data manipulation, individual pieces of information often harmonize to create a more comprehensive melody. Enter records, the versatile and dynamic data structures that allow us to encapsulate and comprehend the interplay between various attributes of an entity. This chapter delves into the world of record functions within Power Query, unraveling the art of transforming raw data into meaningful insights by harnessing the power of structured relationships.

Your journey through this chapter commences with a foundational exploration of records: their anatomy, their attributes, and their capacity to hold a heterogeneous blend of data types. Armed with this understanding, you'll dive into the realm of record creation, discovering how to craft these dynamic containers both manually and through calculated expressions.

Defining a Record

Records are a set of values, each with a specific title, and only one value can be entered for each title. For simplicity, a record can be considered equivalent to a row in a table. To define a record, it needs to first mention the title (like headers in tables) and then show an equal sign and its value between [ ] as follows and as in Figure 7-1:

=[A=123,B=81,C="XYZ"]

© Omid Motamedisedeh 2024
O. Motamedisedeh, *The Ultimate Guide to Functions in Power Query*,
https://doi.org/10.1007/978-1-4842-9754-4_7

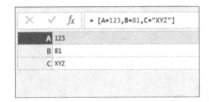

Figure 7-1. *Defining a record in Power Query*

In records, the value of one field can be calculated based on other fields. Therefore, using records, advanced calculations can be done in multiple steps by defining variables. Consider the following and Figure 7-2:

= [A=5,B=A+3,C=A+B]

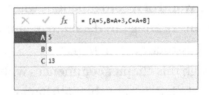

Figure 7-2. *Defining a record*

Each field of a record can be a value, a list, another record, or a table. In the following formula and Figure 7-3, field A is equal to a number, fields B and D are lists, and field C itself is equal to another record:

= [A=5,B={1..3},C=[A=1,B=3],D={2}]

Figure 7-3. *A record containing another record*

As previously explained, records can be considered like a row in a table, so by including the name of the table and then the desired row number within { }, the result is a record in which the field titles are the same as the column titles in the table and the field values are equal to the values of the selected row. For example, consider TableA shown in Table 7-1.

Table 7-1. *TableA*

Product	Price	Material
W11	100	Metal
S06	75	Wood
R08	125	Glass

The value of TableA{0} is equal to the following record:

[Product="W11", Price=100, Material="Metal"]

The value of TableA{2} is equal to the following record:

[Product="R08", Price=125, Material="Glass"]

Due to the nature of the records, mathematical operations (addition, multiplication, division, and subtraction) cannot be performed using operators in Power Query, but two records can be combined using the & operator.

In this case, if two records have the same fields, the value of that field in the last record will be displayed as the result of that field, and different fields will be displayed next to each other in the output. So, the result of the following formula is [A=2, B=3, C=4]. See Figure 7-4.

= [A=5,B=3]&[A=2,C=4]

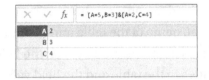

Figure 7-4. Combination of records

In addition to combining records, there are other functions in Power Query to modify records besides those presented in this section.

Record Properties

To extract the number of fields plus their names and values in a record, the below function can be used.

Record.FieldCount

To count the number of fields in a record, `Record.FieldCount` is used as follows:

Record.FieldCount(**record** as record) as number

The result of this function is always a number that displays the number of fields in the input record. Therefore, the result of the following formula is equal to 1:

```
= Record.FieldCount([A=5])
```

And the result of the following formula is equal to 2:

```
= Record.FieldCount([A=5,b=2])
```

And the result of the following formula is 4:

```
= Record.FieldCount([A=5,B={1..3},C=[A=1,B=3],D={2}])
```

Record.FieldNames

Record.FieldNames is used to extract field titles in records as follows:

Record.FieldNames(**record** as record) as list

This function receives a record as input and returns the names of its fields as a list in the output. Therefore, the result of the following formula is {"A", "B"}:

= Record.FieldNames([A=5,B=2])

And the result of the following formula is {"Name", "Family"}:

= Record.FieldNames([Name="Omid",Family="Motamedi"])

Record.FieldValues

Record.FieldValues is like Record.FieldNames, but it results in the values entered in the reference record instead of their title. It is defined as follows:

Record.FieldValues(**record** as record) as list

This function receives a record as input, and its result is equal to a list of values. Therefore, the result of the following formula is equal to {5,2}:

= Record.FieldValues([A=5,B=2])

And the result of the following formula is equal to {"Omid", "Motamedi"}:

= Record.FieldValues([Name="Omid",Family="Motamedi"])

Record.ToList

`Record.ToList` is used to convert a record to a list as follows. This function receives an input in the type of record and displays the values of its fields as a list in the output.

```
Record.ToList(record as record) as list
```

Different examples of using this function are shown in Table 7-2.

Table 7-2. *Examples of Record.ToList*

Formula	Result
= Record.ToList([A=5,B=2,C=10])	{5,2,10}
= Record.ToList([A=5,B={1..3},C=10])	{5,{1,2,3},10}

Record.Field

`Record.Field` is used to extract the value of a field in a record as follows:

```
Record.Field(
        record as record,
        field as text
            ) as any
```

This function receives two inputs as follows:

1. The first input is the reference record.

2. The name of the desired field is determined in the second input in text format.

According to the function explanations, the result of the following formula is equal to 5:

```
= Record.Field([A=5,B=2],"A")
```

And the result of the following formula is equal to Omid:

```
= Record.Field([Name="Omid",Family="Motamedi"],"Name")
```

But since the defined record in the following formula does not include field C, the result of this formula is an error, as shown in Figure 7-5:

```
= Record.Field([A=5,B=2],"C")
```

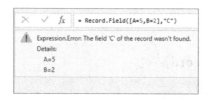

Figure 7-5. *Calculation error*

Record.FieldOrDefault

This function is defined in Power Query as follows:

```
Record.FieldOrDefault(
    record as nullable record,
    field as text,
    optional defaultValue as any
```

This function is like Record.Field. The difference is that in this function, the user can define a value in the third input to display that value instead of an error if the reference record does not include any filed with the defined name in the second input.

Therefore, in the following example, since the defined record does not include field C, the result of the following formula is an error:

```
= Record.Field([A=5,B=2],"C")
```

While the result of the following formula is equal to null:

```
= Record.FieldOrDefault([A=5,B=2],"C")
```

And the output value of the following formula is equal to -1.

```
= Record.FieldOrDefault([A=5,B=2],"C",-1)
```

Record.HasFields

To check if a record contains specific fields, `Record.HasFields` can be used as follows:

```
Record.HasFields(
    record as record,
    fields as any
    ) as logical
```

This function receives two below inputs, and its output is always True if the reference record contains all the defined fields in the second input or False if the defined record does not contain at least one of the field names entered in the second input.

1. The first input is the reference record.

2. The list of field names is entered in the second input. To search for a field, its name can directly enter in the text format, but to search for more than one field, their names should be entered in the list.

Table 7-3 presents different applications of this function.

Table 7-3. *Examples of Record.HasFields*

Formula	Result
= Record.HasFields([A=5,B=2,C={1..4}],"C")	True
= Record.HasFields([A=5,B=2,C={1..4}],"D")	False
= Record.HasFields([A=5,B=2,C={1..4}],{"A","C"})	True
= Record.HasFields([A=5,B=2,C={1..4}],{"A","D"})	False

Record Correction

In this section, the functions for modifying a record will be presented.

Record.AddField

To add a field to a reference record, Record.AddField with the following syntax can be used:

```
Record.AddField(
        record as record,
        fieldName as text,
        value as any,
        optional delayed as nullable logical
                ) as record
```

This function takes the following four inputs:

1. The reference record is entered in the first input.

2. The name of the new field is entered in the second input in the text format.

3. The value of the new field is entered in the third input.

4. The fourth input of this function is optional and is entered as True or False.

Based on the function explanations, to add a new field named C with a value of 10 to a record containing two fields named A and B, the following formula can be used:

```
= Record.AddField([A=5,B=2],"C",10)
```

In this case, the result is a record containing all fields (A, B, and C) as [A=5,B=2,C=10].

Record.Combine

To add more than one field to a record at the same time or to combine several records together, Record.Combine can be used as follows:

```
Record.Combine(records as list) as record
```

To combine several records, all should be entered in a list as the first input of this function. In this case, the result is equal to a record that is obtained by combining all the records.

For example, to combine two records, the following formula can be used, which results in [A=5,B=2,C=10]:

```
= Record.Combine({[A=5,B=2],[C=10]})
```

Similarly, the result of the following formula is equal to [A=5,B=2,C=10,D=2*C,E=1]:

```
= Record.Combine({[A=5,B=2],[C=10,D=
2*C,E=1]})
```

Record.SelectFields

Record.SelectFields is used to extract a subset of a reference record as follows:

```
Record.SelectFields(
        record as record,
        fields as any,
        optional missingField as nullable number
            ) as record
```

This function takes the following three inputs:

1. The first input defines the reference record.

2. The second input is a list of fields that you are searching for their values.

3. This input is optional and used if the reference list does not contain at least one of the mentioned filed names in the second input. By entering the number 0 in this input, the result will be an error. Entering the number 1 will result in a record that the missing fields are removed from. By entering the number 2, the non-matching fields are displayed in the output, but their value is null.

According to the above explanation, the result of the following formula is equal to [A=5,C=10]:

```
Record.SelectFields([A=5,B=2,C=10,D=12],{"A","C"})
```

And the result of the following formula is an error, as shown in Figure 7-6:

```
Record.SelectFields([A=5,B=2,C=10,D=12],{"A","C","N"})
```

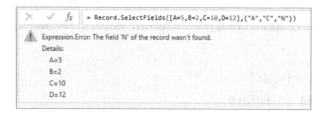

Figure 7-6. *Error result*

However, entering the number 1 in the third input, the result of the following will be as shown in Figure 7-7:

```
Record.SelectFields([A=5,B=2,C=10,D=12],{"A","C","N"},1)
```

Figure 7-7. *Non-matching fields are not displayed*

And entering the number 2 in the third input, the result of the following will be as shown in Figure 7-8:

```
Record.SelectFields([A=5,B=2,C=10,D=12],{"A","C","N"},2)
```

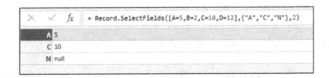

Figure 7-8. *Non-matching fields are displayed with a null value*

Record.RemoveFields

To remove one or more fields from a record, `Record.RemoveFields` is used as follows:

```
Record.RemoveFields(
        record as record,
        fields as any,
        optional missingField as nullable number
            ) as record
```

This function takes the following three inputs:

1. The first input is the reference record.

2. The second input is a list of field names that you want to remove from the reference record. (To remove a field from a record, the field name is inserted in this input in the text format, and to remove more than one field, the field's names should be entered inside a list.)

3. This input is optional and is used when a field name, entered in the second input, does not exist in the reference record. In this case, if the value 0 is entered in this input (or if this input is not entered), the result is an error, and if the numbers 1 or 2 are entered, this inconsistency is ignored.

Based on the function explanations, the result of the following formula is equal to [B=2,C=10,D=20,E=1]:

```
= Record.RemoveFields([A=5,B=2,C=10,D=2*C,E=1],"A")
```

Similarly, the result of the following formula is equal to [D=20,E=1]:

```
= Record.RemoveFields([A=5,B=2,C=10,D=2*C,E=1],
{"A","B","C"})
```

And the result of the following formula is an error:

```
= Record.RemoveFields([A=5,B=2,C=10,D=2*C,E=1],
{"A","B","C","X"})
```

The result of the following formula is equal to [D=20,E=1]:

```
= Record.RemoveFields([A=5,B=2,C=10,D=2*C,E=1],
{"A","B","C","X"},1)
```

Record.RenameFields

Record.RenameFields can be used to change the field names in a record as follows:

```
Record.RenameFields(
       record as record,
       renames as list,
       optional missingField as nullable number
             ) as record
```

This function takes the following three arguments:

1. The reference record is entered in the first input.

2. The old and new names of the fields are entered in this input in the form of a list. To change the name of a field from A to X, the old and new names are entered in a list in the form of {"A","X"}, but to change the name of several fields at the same time, the old and new names are entered separately in lists, and all lists are entered in a list. So, to change the name of field A to X and the name of field B to W, this input enters as {{"A","X"},{"B","W"}}.

3. This input is optional and is used when the reference record does not include any field with the entered name in the second input. In this case, if the value 0 is entered in this input (or if this input is not entered), the result is an error, and if the numbers 1 or 2 are entered, this inconsistency is ignored.

Based on the function explanations, different examples of this function are provided in Table 7-4.

Table 7-4. *Examples of Record.RenameFields*

Formula	Result
= Record.RenameFields([A=5,B=2,C=10],{"A","X"})	[X=5,B=2,C=10]
= Record.RenameFields([A=5,B=2,C=10],{{"A","X"}, {"B","W"}})	[X=5,W=2,C=10]
= Record.RenameFields([A=5,B=2,C=10],{"U","X"})	Error
= Record.RenameFields([A=5,B=2,C=10],{"U","X"},1)	[A=5,B=2,C=10]

Record.ReorderFields

To change the order of fields in a list, Record.ReorderFields can be used as follows:

```
Record.ReorderFields(
        record as record,
        fieldOrder as list,
        optional missingField as nullable number
            ) as record
```

This function takes the following three inputs:

1. In the first input, the reference record is entered.

2. In the second input, the names of the fields are entered in the desired order in a list. In this input, it is not necessary to bring the names of all fields; the mentioned fields' names come in first, and other fields come afterward.

173

3. This input is optional and is used when the reference record does not include any field with the entered name in the second input. In this case, if the value 0 is entered in this input (or if this input is not entered), the result is an error, and if the numbers 1 or 2 are entered, this inconsistency is ignored.

Table 7-5 shows various examples of this function.

Table 7-5. *Examples of Record.ReorderFields*

Formula	Result
= Record.ReorderFields([A=5,B=2,C=10],{"C","B", "A"})	[C=10,B=2,A=5]
= Record.ReorderFields([A=5,B=2,C=10],{"X","B", "A"})	Error
= Record.ReorderFields([A=5,B=2,C=10],{"X","B", "A"},1)	[B=2,C=10,A=5]

Record.TransformFields

With Record.TransformFields, the format of values in a record can be changed as follows:

```
Record.TransformFields(
        record as record,
        transformOperations as list,
        optional missingField as nullable number
            ) as record
```

This function takes the following three arguments:

1. The first argument represents the reference record.

2. The names of the fields, beside their new format, are entered in a different list. This input is defined as a list including two values, first, define the name of the column, and the logic for transforming is defined in the second input.

3. This input is optional, and by using it, you specify what happens if the reference record does not include any field with the names listed in the second input.

Using this function, the result of the following formula is [A="4", B=4, C=4]:

```
Record.TransformFields([A="4", B=4, C="4"], {C, Number.
FromText})
```

Record Conversion

Here are several functions in Power Query for converting a record to a list or table.

Record.FromList

As the name of this function suggests, it is used to convert a list to a record as follows:

```
Record.FromList(
        list as list,
        fields as any
                ) as record
```

This function takes two inputs as follows, and its output is always equal to a record.

1. In the first input of this function, the field values are entered as a list.

2. In the second input of this function, the field names are entered as a list.

Based on the function explanation, various uses of this function are shown in Table 7-6.

Table 7-6. *Examples of Record.FromList*

Formula	Result
`= Record.FromList({1,2,3},{"A","B","C"})`	[A=1,B=2,C=3]
`= Record.FromList({1,"XWZ",3},{"A","B","C"})`	[A=1,B="XWZ",C=3]
`= Record.FromList({1,2,3},type` `[A=number,B=number,C=number])`	[A=1,B=2,C=3]

Record.FromTable

Using `Record.FromTable`, tables with specific conditions can be converted to records as follows:

`Record.FromTable(`**`table`** `as table) as record`

As you can see, this function receives an input in the type of table and converts it to the record. To use this function, the input table must include two columns. The first column contains values in the format of text. Then, in the output record, the values of the first column of the reference table are considered as the field names, and the values of the second column in the table are considered as the values of the output.

Record.ToTable

By using `Record.ToTable`, a record can be transformed into a table as follows:

`Record.ToTable(`**`record`**` as record) as table`

This function receives an input of the record type and transforms the same record into a two-column table according to the following format. The first column of the table includes the names of record fields, and the second column includes the values of the fields. See Figure 7-9.

Figure 7-9. *Transforming a record into a table*

Summary

This chapter was a comprehensive exploration of record functions within Power Query, offering a deep dive into the art of transforming raw data into meaningful insights by harnessing the power of structured relationships.

The journey began with a foundational understanding of records as dynamic data structures. You learned about their ability to encapsulate various attributes of an entity, akin to creating multidimensional canvases for data representation. Through this, you gained insight into the manual creation of records and generating them through calculated expressions.

The true essence of record functions emerged as you unraveled their capabilities in data transformation and enrichment. You explored a diverse range of functions that empower you to dissect, merge, and reshape records. From filtering attributes and extracting values to merging records to create holistic data snapshots, you learned to mold data with precision.

In the next chapter, you continue your journey by learning about the functions related to tables, as the most important type of data in Power Query. You will learn how to merge the values in several separate tables and how to append them or modify the single tables.

CHAPTER 8

Tables

In the sprawling landscape of data exploration and analysis, tables stand as the cornerstone of structure and coherence. They organize chaos, provide context, and facilitate insights by presenting data in a logical and digestible format. Welcome to a chapter that delves into the intricate world of table functions within Power Query, guiding you through the art of transforming raw information into organized, actionable knowledge.

Tables are the canvases upon which data stories unfold. Imagine customer orders neatly categorized, project tasks meticulously tracked, or survey responses collated for analysis. In a world of disparate data points, tables are the glue that holds information together, facilitating seamless exploration and understanding.

Your journey through this chapter begins with a fundamental understanding of tables: their anatomy, their columns, and their rows of data. You'll explore how Power Query views tables as dynamic structures capable of housing diverse data types and relationships. Armed with this knowledge, you'll embark on a journey to create tables manually and through calculated expressions.

However, tables are not static entities; they are pathways to transformation and enlightenment. Discover the myriad table functions that Power Query provides, enabling you to filter, sort, reshape, and aggregate data with precision. From column removal to row filtering, these functions empower you to craft tables that align with your analytical goals.

© Omid Motamedisedeh 2024
O. Motamedisedeh, *The Ultimate Guide to Functions in Power Query*,
https://doi.org/10.1007/978-1-4842-9754-4_8

Creating a Table

There are various methods in Power Query to create or call tables from different data sources. This section covers creating a table from a record, list, rows, or columns using the following functions.

Table.FromColumns

As the name of this function suggests, `Table.FromColumns` is used to create a table from a set of columns, as follows:

```
Table.FromColumns(
            lists as list,
            optional columns as any
            ) as table
```

This function receives these two inputs:

1. The first input of this function represents the contents of the columns in the desired table, where the values of each column are entered in a list and all lists are entered in a reference list in this input. In other words, entering {{1,2},{3,4}} in this input means that the desired table has two columns where the first column includes values of 1 and 2 and the second column includes values of 3 and 4.

2. The second input of this function is optional and specifies the column's titles. In this input, the column's titles are entered in a list. If no value is entered for this input, 1, Column 2, ... are used for the name of outputted table.

Based on the function explanation, to create a table with three columns, its first input is a list that includes three other lists. Each inner list includes the values related to a column of the table. The second input of the table also includes a list that has three text values as the header of the columns. So, the result of the following formula is equal to a table with three columns and two rows, as follows and as shown in Table 8-1:

```
= Table.FromColumns(
        {
                {"Omid","Ali"},
                {"Motamedi","Amjad"},
                {31,35}
        },
        {"Name","Family","Age"})
```

Table 8-1. *Creating a Table by Table.FromColumns*

Name	Family	Age
Omid	Motamedi	31
Ali	Amjad	35

In a similar state, the result of the following formula is equal to Table 8-2:

```
= Table.FromColumns(
        {
                {"Omid"},
                {null,"Amjad"},
                {"",35}
        },
        {"Name","Family","Age"})
```

Table 8-2. *Creating a Table by Table.FromColumns*

Name	Family	Age
Omid	null	
null	Amjad	35

And if the information related to the second input is not entered, as in the following formula, the columns are named column 1, column 2, and column3 and result is as shown in Table 8-3:

```
= Table.FromColumns({{"Omid","Ali"},{"Motamedi","Amjad"},
{31,35}})
```

Table 8-3. *Creating a Table by Table.FromColumns*

Column1	Column2	Column3
Omid	Motamedi	31
Ali	Amjad	35

Table.FromRows

The `Table.FromRows` function is like the `Table.FromColumns` function. The difference is that in the first input of this function, instead of defining the columns' values of the table, the values corresponding to the rows are defined as follows:

```
Table.FromRows(
            rows as list,
            optional columns as any
            ) as table
```

This function receives these two inputs:

1. The first input is a list that includes several lists, each list containing the rows' values. In other words, if the value {{1,2},{3,4}} is entered in this input, it means that the desired table has two rows and the values 1 and 2 are entered in the first row and the values 3 and 4 are entered in the second row.

2. The headers of the table are defined in a list within this input. This input is optional and if not entered, the column titles will be displayed as Column 1, Column 2, and so on.

Based on the function explanation, the result of the following formula is a table with three columns and two rows, as shown in Table 8-4:

```
= Table.FromRows(
        {
                {"Omid","Motamedi",31},
                {"Ali","Amjad",35}
        },
        {"Name","Family","age"}
                )
```

Table 8-4. *Creating a Table by Table.FromRows*

Name	Family	age
Omid	Motamedi	31
Ali	Amjad	35

And if the second input is not entered, the result will be as shown in Table 8-5.

```
= Table.FromRows(
        {
                {"Omid","Motamedi",31},
                {"Ali","Amjad",35}
        })
```

Table 8-5. *Creating a Table by Table.FromRows*

Column1	Column2	Column3
Omid	Motamedi	31
Ali	Amjad	35

In a similar situation, if some values are not available, you can replace them with the null expression or leave them empty, as shown here and in Table 8-6:

```
= Table.FromRows({{"Omid","",""},{null,"Amjad",35}},{"Name",
"Family","age"})
```

Table 8-6. *Creating a Table by Table.FromRows*

Name	Family	age
Omid		
null	Amjad	35

Table.FromRecords

Table.FromRecords is used to create a table from a set of records. In this function, each record presents a row of the table and the records must be entered into a list as the first input of this function. The fields of the records can be the same or different, but in the second input of this function, you specify which fields should be displayed in the output. In the third input of this function, you specify how to calculate the values of a field if no value is entered. This function is defined as follows:

```
Table.FromRecords(
        records as list,
        optional columns as any,
        optional missingField as nullable number
        ) as table
```

This function receives these three inputs:

1. In this input, the values of the table rows are defined. The values of each row are entered in a record and all records are defined in a list as the first input.

2. This input is optional and is used to display only specific fields of the records entered in the first input in the final table. The names of those fields can be entered in a list in this input. Otherwise, by not entering a value for this input, all fields of the records will be displayed in the output.

3. The third input of this function is also optional and specifies how to calculate the values of a field that is defined in the second input but none of the records in the first input include that field. In this

input, one of three states of MissingField.Error
(or value 0), MissingField.Ignore (or value 1), and
MissingField.UseNull (or value 2) can be used.

Based on the function explanation, the result of the following formula
is shown in Table 8-7:

```
= Table.FromRecords(
        {[Name="Omid",Family="Motamedi",Age=31],
         [Name="Ali",Family="Amjad",Age=35]}
    )
```

Table 8-7. *Creating a Table by Table.FromRecords*

Name	Family	Age
Omid	Motamedi	31
Ali	Amjad	35

And by specifying some column names like Name and Age in the
second input, the result will change, as shown in Table 8-8.

```
= Table.FromRecords(
        {[Name="Omid",Family="Motamedi",Age=31],
         [Name="Ali",Family="Amjad",Age=35]},
        {"Name","Age"})
```

Table 8-8. *Creating a Table by Table.FromRecords*

Name	Age
Omid	31
Ali	35

If the second record does not include the Name field, the result of the following formula will look like Table 8-9:

```
= Table.FromRecords(
        {[Name="Omid",Family="Motamedi",Age=31],
         [Family="Amjad",Age=35]},
        {"Name","Age"})
```

Table 8-9. *Creating a Table by Table.FromRecords*

Name	Age
Omid	31
Error	Error

In this case, by entering the number 2 in the third input of the function, the result will be as shown in Table 8-10.

Table 8-10. *Creating a Table by Table.FromRecords*

Name	Age
Omid	31
null	35

Table.FromValue

Using Table.FromValue, values with different formats can be converted to a table as follows:

```
Table.FromValue(
        value as any,
        optional options as nullable record
              ) as table
```

As you can see, this function receives the following two inputs:

1. In the first input of this function, the values you want to convert to a table are entered. These value can be in the form of a number, list, record, or other formats.

2. The second input of this function is optional and contains settings related to the function. For example, using DefaultColumnName, the column name of the table can be changed.

If a list is used in the first input as = Table.FromValue({"A",2,3}), the resulting table is as shown in Table 8-11.

Table 8-11. *Creating a Table by Table.FromValue*

Value
A
2
3

If the record is used as = Table.FromValue([a=1,b=2,c=3]), the result table is as shown in Table 8-12.

Table 8-12. *Creating a Table by Table.FromValue*

Name	Value
a	1
b	2
c	3

And if a numerical or textual value is entered, the table is as shown in Table 8-13.

```
= Table.FromValue(2)
```

Table 8-13. *Creating a Table by Table.FromValue*

Value
2

Table Conversion

Using Power Query functions, a table can be converted into a list, record, columns, or rows. In this section, these kinds of functions are examined. For simplicity, Table 8-14 is considered as TableA and is used in the several example.

Table 8-14. *Definition of Table A*

Product	Price	Material
W11	100	Metal
S06	75	Wood
R08	125	Glass

And Table 8-15 is considered as TableB.

Table 8-15. *Definition of TableB*

Name	Family	Age
Omid	Motamedi	31
Ali	Amjad	35

Table.ToRecords

Using Table.ToRecords with the following syntax, a table can be converted to a set of records:

Table.ToRecords(**table** as table) as list

This function takes an input of type table, and its output is a list where each of its values represents a record that corresponds to a row of the original table values.

With these explanations, the result of the formula Table. ToRecords(TableB) is equal to the following list:

{[Name="Omid",Family="Motamedi",Age=31],
[Name="Ali",Family="Amjad",Age=35]}

And the result of the formula Table.ToRecords(TableA) is equal to the following list:

{[Product="W11",Price=100,Material="Metal"],
[Product="S06",Price=75,Material="Wood"],
[Product="R08",Price=125,Material="Glass"]}

Table.ToColumns

The Table.ToColumns function with the following syntax can be used to convert the table's column values into lists:

Table.ToColumns(**table** as table) as list

Using this function, each column of a table is converted to a list, and all lists are displayed as the values of other lists as output. In other words, this function takes an input of the type of table, and its output is a list that includes a list for each column of the reference table. So, the result of the formula Table.ToColumns(TableB) is equal to the following list:

```
{{ "Omid","Ali"},
{ "Motamedi","Amjad"},
{31, 35}}
```

And the result of the formula `Table.ToColumns(TableA)` is equal to the following list:

```
{{ "W11", "S06", "R08"},
{100, 75, 125},
{"Metal", "Wood", "Glass"}}
```

Table.ToRows

Using `Table.ToRows`, a table can be converted to a set of rows where each row is displayed within a list. In other words, this function receives an input in the format of a table and its output is equal to a list where each of its values represents a list that is equivalent to a row of the original table.

The syntax of this function is as follows:

```
Table.ToRows(table as table) as list
```

So, the result of the formula `Table.ToRows(TableB)` is equal to the following list:

```
{{ "Omid","Motamedi", 31},
{ "Ali","Amjad", 35}}
```

And the result of the formula `Table.ToRows(TableA)` is equal to the following list:

```
{{ "W11", 100, "Metal"},
{ "S06", 75, "Wood"},
{ "R08", 125, "Glass"}}
```

Table.ToList

Table.ToList is used to convert a table to a list as follows:

```
Table.ToList(
    table as table,
    optional combiner as nullable function
        ) as list
```

This function receives these two inputs:

1. The first input is the reference table.

2. The second input of this function is optional and specifies the type of combining values of different columns by entering one of these values:

   Combiner.CombineTextByDelimiter

   Combiner.CombineTextByEachDelimiter

   Combiner.CombineTextByLengths

   Combiner.CombineTextByPositions

   Combiner.CombineTextByRanges

An important point about this function is that before using it, the format of all columns of the reference table must be changed to text.

By considering TableA as shown in Table 8-13, and assuming that the column format in the Price column is defined as text, the result of formula = Table.ToList(TableA) is equal to the list {"W11,100,Metal", "S06,75,Wood", "R08,125,Glass"}.

In addition, the following formula states that the first, second, and third columns of TableA should be combined together by taking 1, 2, and 2 first characters of each column, respectively. Therefore, the result is {"W10Me", "S75Wo", "R12Gl"}:

```
= Table.ToList(TableA, Combiner.CombineTextByLengths({1,2,2}))
```

In the following example, the dash is the separator:

```
= Table.ToList(TableA, Combiner.CombineTextByDelimiter("-"))
```

Therefore, the result of the above formula is equal to

```
{"W11-100-Metal", "S06-75-Wood", "R08-125-Glass"}
```

And by using `Combiner.CombineTextByEachDelimiter` as follows, a different separator can be defined for combining the columns.

```
= Table.ToList(TableA, Combiner.
CombineTextByEachDelimiter({".","_"}))
```

So the result is

```
{"W11.100-Metal", "S06.75-Wood", "R08.125-Glass"}
```

Table.Column

Using `Table.Column` with the following syntax, the values of a column can be extracted as a list:

```
Table.Column(
        table as table,
        column as text
            ) as list
```

This function receives these two inputs:

1. The first input of this function specifies the reference table.

2. The second input of this function is the name of the desired column as text.

The result of this function is a list that includes the values of the specified column in the second input. Therefore, the result of Table.Column(TableC, "Quantity") is equal to this list:

{17,18,10,1,6,9,6,6,10,3,18}

In addition to Table.Column, to extract the values of a column from a table, the name of the column can be written in [ ] after the table name. Therefore, the result of TableC[Quantity] is also equal to the values of the Quantity column, just like Table.Column(TableC, "Quantity").

Table.TransformRows

With the function Table.TransformRows, you can transform values in the rows of a table into a list as follows:

```
Table.TransformRows(
        table as table,
        transform as function
            ) as list
```

Based on the function's syntax, it takes these two inputs:

1. The first input of this function is the reference table.

2. The second input defines the transformation function to convert the values into a list.

By this function, the values of the table are converted into a list based on the transformation function defined in the second input. For example, the result of the following formula is equal to the list {100, 75, 125}:

```
= Table.TransformRows(TableA, each [Price])
```

And the result of following formula is equal to {"W11, Metal", "S06, Wood", "R08, Glass"}:

```
= Table.TransformRows(TableA, each [Product] & ", " &
[Material])
```

In the following example, the first character of the product name and the last character of the product material should be displayed next to each other in the output list. The result is {"Wl", "Sd", "Rs"}:

```
= Table.TransformRows(TableA, each Text.Start([Product], 1) &
Text.End([Material], 1))
```

Table.Split

Table.Split is used to split a table into multiple tables. For example, with this function a table with 100 rows can be split into 50 tables with 2 rows.

```
Table.Split(
    table as tle,
    pageSize as number
) as list
```

This function takes two arguments:

1. The first argument is the reference table.

2. The second argument determines the number of rows in the split tables. For example, to split a table with 100 rows into 50 tables with 2 rows, 2 is entered in this input.

The output of this function is a list where each value of it is a sub-table of the original table.

According to the above explanation, by considering X as a table with 11 rows, the result of the formula `Table.Split(X,2)` is a list with 6 values. The first 5 values of this list are tables with 2 rows, and the sixth value is a table with 1 row.

Table.SplitAt

`Table.SplitAt` is used to divide a table into two sub-tables based on a criteria.

```
Table.SplitAt(
     table as table,
     count as number
     ) as list
```

This function receives two inputs:

1. The first input is the reference table.

2. In this input, the location of the table split is determined. In other words, entering the number 3 in this input means that the reference table is divided into two subsets. The first four rows will be shown in the first table and the remaining rows will be in the second table.

So, by considering X as a table with 11 rows, the result of the formula `Table.SplitAt(X,3)` is a list with two values. The first value is a table containing the first four rows of the reference table, and the second value is a table containing the remaining rows of the reference table.

Information

There are several functions in Power Query that provide information such as the number of columns and rows in a table. These functions receive an input in the form of a table and provide information about that table in the output. Table 8-16 lists of these functions along with their applications.

Table 8-16. *Table Information Functions*

Function	Description
Table.Approximate RowCount	The result of this function is equal to the approximate number of rows in a large table (if the relevant database follows this feature).
Table.ColumnCount	The output of this function is equal to the number of columns in the input table.
Table.IsEmpty	If the table defined in the input of this function has no rows, the result of this function is True; otherwise, the result of the function is False.
Table.Profile	The result of this function is equal to a table that provides statistical information, including minimum, maximum, mean, standard deviation, number of records, number of unique records, and number of null values for different columns of the input table.
Table.RowCount	The result of this function is equal to the number of rows in the reference table.
Table.Schema	The result of this function is a table that provides additional information about the columns of the reference table.

Considering Table 8-14 named TableA and Table 8-15 named TableB, Table 8-17 shows the results of using various formulas.

Table 8-17. *Examples of Table Information Functions*

Formula	Result
=Table.ColumnCount(TableB)	3
=Table.IsEmpty (TableB)	False
=Table.RowCount(TableB)	2
=Table.ColumnCount(TableA)	3
=Table.IsEmpty (TableA)	False
=Table.RowCount(TableA)	3

And the result of the function `Table.Profile(TableB)` is equal to Table 8-18.

Table 8-18. *Result of Table.Profile*

Column	Min	Max	Average	StandardDeviation	Count	NullCount	DistinctCount
Age	31	35	33	2.828427125	2	0	2
Family	Amjad	Motamedi	null	null	2	0	2
Name	Ali	Omid	null	null	2	0	2

Selecting Table Rows

Using various functions in Power Query, the number of desired rows can be extracted from a table. These functions are explained in this section. To examine the functions in this section, Table 8-19 is considered TableC.

```
= Table.FromColumns(
        {{1,2,3,4,5,6,7,8,9,10,11},
        {#date(2023,1,30),#date(2023,1,31),#date(2023,2,1),
        #date(2023,2,1),#date(2023,2,1),#date(2023,2,2),#date
        (2023,2,2),#date(2023,2,3),#date(2023,2,4),#date
        (2023,2,4),#date(2023,2,6)},
        {"A","A","C","A","B","B","A","C","B","A","C"},
        {17,18,10,1,6,9,6,6,10,3,18}},
        {"Row","Date","Product Name","Quantity"})
```

Table 8-19. *Definition of TableC*

Row	Date	Product Name	Quantity
1	1/30/2023	A	17
2	1/31/2023	A	18
3	2/1/2023	C	10
4	2/1/2023	A	1
5	2/1/2023	B	6
6	2/2/2023	B	9
7	2/2/2023	A	6
8	2/3/2023	C	6
9	2/4/2023	B	10
10	2/4/2023	A	3
11	2/6/2023	C	18

Table.FirstValue

The result of Table.FirstValue is always equal to the value entered in the first row and first column of a table. Table.FirstValue is defined as follows in Power Query:

```
Table.FirstValue(
    table as table,
    optional default as any
        ) as any
```

Based on the function syntax, it takes two inputs:

1. The first input of this function specifies the reference table.

2. The second input of this function is optional. This input represents the default value of this function, and if the result of the function is an error (the table entered in the first input is empty), this value will display.

Table.First and Table.Last

Table.First and Table.Last are used to extract the first or last row of a table as follows:

```
Table.First(
    table as table,
    optional default as any
    ) as any
```

```
Table.Last(
    table as table,
    optional default as any
    ) as any
```

These functions take two arguments, as follows:

1. The first argument is the reference table.

2. The second argument of this function is optional
    and can be used to determine what value should
    be displayed in the output if the first input of the
    function is empty (the reference table has no rows).

The result of these functions is always a record that displays the values
of the first or last row of the reference table. Therefore, the result of the
formula Table.First(TableC) is as follows:

[Row=1,Date="1/30/2023",Product Name=A,Quantity=17]

And similarly, the result of the function Table.Last(TableC) is as
follows:

[Row=11,Date="2/6/2023",Product Name=C,Quantity=18]

Table.FirstN and Table.LastN

Table.FirstN and Table.LastN are used to extract several rows from the
beginning or ending of a table as follows:

```
Table.FirstN(
        table as table,
        countOrCondition as any
        ) as table
```

```
Table.LastN(
        table as table,
        countOrCondition as any
        ) as table
```

Based on the syntaxes, they take two inputs:

1. The first input is the reference table.

2. In the second input of this function, the number n is entered and determines how many rows should be extracted from the beginning or ending the table. In this input, a condition can also be defined; in this case, only a chain of first (or last) rows of the table that meet this condition will be displayed in the output table.

With these explanations, the result of the formula `Table.FirstN(TableC,5)` is as shown in Table 8-20.

***Table 8-20.** Example of Table.FirstN*

Row	Date	Product Name	Quantity
1	1/30/2023	A	17
2	1/31/2023	A	18
3	2/1/2023	C	10
4	2/1/2023	A	1
5	2/1/2023	B	6

The result of the formula = `Table.FirstN(TableC, each [Quantity]>9)` is equal to Table 8-21.

***Table 8-21.** Example of Table.FirstN*

Row	Date	Product Name	Quantity
1	1/30/2023	A	17
2	1/31/2023	A	18
3	2/1/2023	C	10

Similarly, the result of the formula `Table.LastN(TableC,5)` is as shown in Table 8-22.

Table 8-22. Example of Table.FirstN

Row	Date	Product Name	Quantity
7	2/2/2023	A	6
8	2/3/2023	C	6
9	2/4/2023	B	10
10	2/4/2023	A	3
11	2/6/2023	C	18

And the result of the formula = `Table.LastN(TableC, each [Quantity]>9)` is equal to Table 8-23.

Table 8-23. Example of Table.FirstN

Row	Date	Product Name	Quantity
11	2/6/2023	C	18

Table.Max and Table.Min

`Table.Max` and `Table.Min` are used to extract a row from a table that includes the largest or smallest value in the specified column.

```
Table.Max(
    table as table,
    comparisonCriteria as any,
    optional default as any
    ) as any
```

```
Table.Min(
table as table,
comparisonCriteria as any,
optional default as any
        ) as any
```

The functions `Table.Max` and `Table.Min` each receive three inputs:

1. The first input of these functions is the reference table.

2. In this input, the comparison criterion is specified. Usually, the name of the column in which you are searching for the largest or smallest value is directly entered in this input as a text format.

3. The third input is optional and specifies the default value of the function; for the case the result of functions is an error.

According to the above explanation, to extract the row corresponding to the minimum sales in TableC, the following formula can be used:

```
= Table.Min(TableC, "Quantity")
```

In this case, the result is shown in Figure 8-1.

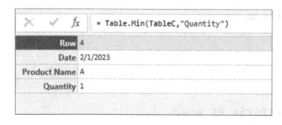

Figure 8-1. *The row corresponding to the minimum sales*

To extract the row corresponding to the maximum sales, the following formula can be used:

```
= Table.Max(TableC, "Quantity")
```

The result is shown in Figure 8-2. (Although there is a row with the sale value of 18, the result of this function is only one of these rows.)

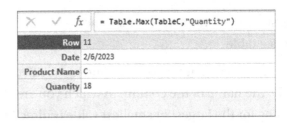

Figure 8-2. *Row corresponding to the maximum sales*

Table.MaxN and Table.MinN

`Table.MaxN` and `Table.MinN` are used to extract N rows corresponding to the largest or smallest values for a column in a table, as follows:

```
Table.MaxN(
        table as table,
        comparisonCriteria as any,
        countOrCondition as any
        ) as table
```

```
Table.MinN(
        table as table,
        comparisonCriteria as any,
        countOrCondition as any
        ) as table
```

These functions receive three inputs as follows:

1. The first input is the reference table.

2. The title of the desired column in which you are searching for the n largest (smallest) values is entered in the second input.

3. In the third input, the number of rows is specified.

Based on the function explanation, the result of the formula = `Table.MaxN(TableC,"Quantity",3)` is equal to the three rows of the table with the highest sales value. See Table 8-24.

Table 8-24. *Result of Table.MaxN(TableC,"Quantity",3)*

Row	Date	Product Name	Quantity
11	2/6/2023	C	18
2	1/31/2023	A	18
1	1/30/2023	A	17

Similarly, formula = `Table.MinN(TableC,"Quantity",3)` results in three rows of the table with the lowest value in the quantity column. See Table 8-25.

Table 8-25. *Result of Table.MinN(TableC,"Quantity",3)*

Row	Date	Product Name	Quantity
4	2/1/2023	A	1
10	2/4/2023	A	3
8	2/3/2023	C	6

Table.Range

To extract n rows from the middle rows of a table, `Table.Range` can be used as follows:

```
Table.Range(
        table as table,
        offset as number,
        optional count as nullable number
        ) as table
```

This function takes three arguments:

1. In the first argument, the reference table is entered.

2. In the second argument, by entering a number, the starting point for extracting the rows is determined. For example, entering the number 3 means that separation will take place from the fourth row of the table.

3. In the third argument of this function, the number of rows for extracting is determined by entering a number.

Therefore, entering `Table.Range(TableC,3,5)` means rows 4 to 8 of TableC will be extracted. The result is shown in Table 8-26.

Table 8-26. *Result of Table.Range(TableC,3,5)*

Row	Date	Product Name	Quantity
4	2/1/2023	A	1
5	2/1/2023	B	6
6	2/2/2023	B	9
7	2/2/2023	A	6
8	2/3/2023	C	6

Table.SelectRows

Table.SelectRows with the following syntax allows you to filter some rows of a table based on the condition:

```
Table.SelectRows(
      table as table,
      condition as function
           ) as table
```

Table.SelectRows takes two inputs, and its result is always a table with filtered rows from the reference table.

1. In the first input of this function, the reference table is entered.

2. In the second input, the condition(s) for selecting rows is defined in the format of function. In the simplest way, the word "each" can be entered, followed by the selecting condition. For example, to filter only the rows with the value "A" in the Product Name column, the second input of this function can be entered as each [Product Name] = "A".

To display only the rows with values higher than 10 on the quantity column, this input is defined as each [Quantity]>10.

Based on the function explanation and considering TableC, the result of this function in different conditions is as follows (see also Table 8-27 and Table 8-28):

```
= Table.SelectRows(TableC, each [Product Name] = "A")
```

Table 8-27. *Example of Table.SelectRows*

Row	Date	Product Name	Quantity
1	1/30/2023	A	17
2	1/31/2023	A	18
4	2/1/2023	A	1
7	2/2/2023	A	6
10	2/4/2023	A	3

```
= Table.SelectRows(TableC,each [Quantity]>10)
```

Table 8-28. *Example of Table.SelectRows*

Row	Date	Product Name	Quantity
1	1/30/2023	A	17
2	1/31/2023	A	18
11	2/6/2023	C	18

To execute more than one condition at the same time, the conditions are connected by using "and" or "or" between them, as follows:

```
= Table.SelectRows(TableC,each [Product Name]="A" and
[Quantity]>10)
```

This means that only the rows related to the sales of product A with more than 10 items on the quantity column will be displayed in the output. (Both conditions must be met simultaneously.) See Table 8-29.

Table 8-29. *Example of Table.SelectRows*

Row	Date	Product Name	Quantity
1	1/30/2023	A	17
2	1/31/2023	A	18

In another example, replacing "and" by "or" means that all rows where product A has been sold should be displayed alongside all rows where more than 10 units of the product have been sold (at least one of the conditions must be met). See Table 8-30.

```
= Table.SelectRows(TableC,each [Product Name]="A" or
[Quantity]>10)
```

Table 8-30. *Example of Table.SelectRows*

Row	Date	Product Name	Quantity
1	1/30/2023	A	17
2	1/31/2023	A	18
4	2/1/2023	A	1
7	2/2/2023	A	6
10	2/4/2023	A	3
11	2/6/2023	C	18

Table.SelectRowsWithErrors

Table.SelectRowsWithErrors is used to find rows in a table with error values in at least one column. This function is defined in Power Query as follows:

```
Table.SelectRows(
        table as table,
        condition as function
            ) as table
```

Based on the function syntax, it takes two inputs:

1. The reference table is entered in the first input.

2. In the second input of this function, the names of columns are entered as a list. This input is optional, and if a list of column names is entered, the output of this function will include the table's rows with an error value in the columns mentioned in this input. If no value is entered for this input, all the columns are considered for extracting rows with the error value.

For example, consider Table 8-31 as TableD.

Table 8-31. *Definition of TableD*

Row	Date	Product Name	Quantity
1	1/30/2023	A	17
2	1/31/2023	A	18
3	2/1/2023	C	Error
4	2/1/2023	A	1
5	2/1/2023	B	6
6	2/2/2023	B	9
7	2/2/2023	A	6
8	2/3/2023	C	Error
9	2/4/2023	Error	10
10	2/4/2023	A	3
11	2/6/2023	C	Error

The result of the formula `Table.SelectRowsWithErrors(TableD)` is shown in Table 8-32.

Table 8-32. *Example of Table.SelectRowsWithErrors*

Row	Date	Product Name	Quantity
3	2/1/2023	C	Error
8	2/3/2023	C	Error
9	2/4/2023	Error	10
11	2/6/2023	C	Error

And the result of = `Table.SelectRowsWithErrors(TableD,{"Product Name"})` is shown in Table 8-33.

Table 8-33. Example of Table.SelectRowsWithError

Row	Date	Product Name	Quantity
9	2/4/2023	Error	10

Deleting Table Rows

To remove one or more rows of a table, the following functions can be used.

Table.RemoveFirstN and Table.RemoveLastN

The two functions `Table.RemoveFirstN` and `Table.RemoveLastN` are used to remove a specified number of rows from the beginning or end of a table, as follows:

```
Table.RemoveFirstN(
    table as table,
    optional countOrCondition as any
    ) as table
```

```
Table.RemoveLastN(
    table as table,
    optional countOrCondition as any
    ) as table
```

These functions take two inputs:

1. The first input is the reference table.

2. The second input is the number of rows you want to remove from the beginning or end of the reference table, entered as a number or condition.

The result of the formula `Table.RemoveFirstN(TableC,5)` is shown in Table 8-34.

Table 8-34. *Result of Table.RemoveFirstN*

Row	Date	Product Name	Quantity
6	2/2/2023	B	9
7	2/2/2023	A	6
8	2/3/2023	C	6
9	2/4/2023	B	10
10	2/4/2023	A	3
11	2/6/2023	C	18

Similarly, the result of the formula `Table.RemoveFirstN(TableC,` each [Quantity]>9) is shown in Table 8-35.

Table 8-35. *Result of Table.RemoveFirstN*

Row	Date	Product Name	Quantity
4	2/1/2023	A	1
5	2/1/2023	B	6
6	2/2/2023	B	9
7	2/2/2023	A	6
8	2/3/2023	C	6
9	2/4/2023	B	10
10	2/4/2023	A	3
11	2/6/2023	C	18

And the result of the formula `Table.RemoveLastN(TableC,5)` is shown in Table 8-36.

Table 8-36. *Result of Table.RemoveFirstN*

Row	Date	Product Name	Quantity
1	1/30/2023	A	17
2	1/31/2023	A	18
3	2/1/2023	C	10
4	2/1/2023	A	1
5	2/1/2023	B	6
6	2/2/2023	B	9

Similarly, the result of the formula = `Table.RemoveLastN(TableC, each [Quantity]>9)` is shown in Table 8-37.

Table 8-37. *Result of Table.RemoveFirstN*

Row	Date	Product Name	Quantity
1	1/30/2023	A	17
2	1/31/2023	A	18
3	2/1/2023	C	10
4	2/1/2023	A	1
5	2/1/2023	B	6
6	2/2/2023	B	9
7	2/2/2023	A	6
8	2/3/2023	C	6
9	2/4/2023	B	10
10	2/4/2023	A	3

Table.Distinct

To remove duplicate rows in a table, `Table.Distinct` can be used as follows:

```
Table.Distinct(
        table as table,
        optional equationCriteria as any
            ) as table
```

This function receives two inputs, and if there are duplicate rows based on the conditions defined in the second input, all duplicate rows except the first one are removed from the reference table.

1. The first input is the reference table.

2. This input is optional and allows the user to specify custom criteria for comparing the values. For example, if you are entering a list of column names, the search for duplicate rows can be limited to the limited columns, instead of the whole table.

Considering TableC, the following formula states that duplicate rows should be removed based on the Product Name column (rows with the same product name are identified as duplicates):

```
= Table.Distinct(TableC,"Product Name")
```

Therefore, regardless of the values entered in other columns, only the first row for each product will be displayed in the output, and other rows will be removed. The result of the above formula is shown in Table 8-38.

Table 8-38. *Result of Table.Distinct*

Row	Date	Product Name	Quantity
1	1/30/2023	A	17
3	2/1/2023	C	10
5	2/1/2023	B	6

In a similar situation, to consider the values in the Date column for evaluation of duplicate rows, the following formula can be used:

```
= Table.Distinct(TableC,"Date")
```

The result of this formula are shown in Table 8-39.

Table 8-39. *Result of Table.Distinct*

Row	Date	Product Name	Quantity
1	1/30/2023	A	17
2	1/31/2023	A	18
3	2/1/2023	C	10
6	2/2/2023	B	9
8	2/3/2023	C	6
9	2/4/2023	B	10
11	2/6/2023	C	18

And to consider all columns for determining duplicate rows, the following formula can be used. The result is TableC (because there was no repetitive data in the reference table). See Table 8-40.

```
= Table.Distinct(TableC,"Date")
```

Table 8-40. *Result of Table.Distinct*

Row	Date	Product Name	Quantity
1	1/30/2023	A	17
2	1/31/2023	A	18
3	2/1/2023	C	10
4	2/1/2023	A	1
5	2/1/2023	B	6
6	2/2/2023	B	9
7	2/2/2023	A	6
8	2/3/2023	C	6
9	2/4/2023	B	10
10	2/4/2023	A	3
11	2/6/2023	C	18

Table.Skip

Table.Skip is very like Table.RemoveFirstN and is used to remove a number of rows from the beginning of a table as follows:

```
Table.Skip(
    table as table,
    optional countOrCondition as any
) as table
```

This function receives two inputs:

1. The first input of this function is the reference table.

2. In the second input of this function, the number of rows that you want to remove from the beginning of the table or the condition for removing the initial rows is entered. This input is optional; if not entered, only the first row of the reference table is removed. If a number such as 4 is entered, the first four rows are removed. If a condition is defined, the initial rows of the table that meet that condition are removed.

So, the result of the formula `Table.Skip(TableC,3)` is as shown in Table 8-41.

Table 8-41. *Result of Table.Skip*

Row	Date	Product Name	Quantity
4	2/1/2023	A	1
5	2/1/2023	B	6
6	2/2/2023	B	9
7	2/2/2023	A	6
8	2/3/2023	C	6
9	2/4/2023	B	10
10	2/4/2023	A	3
11	2/6/2023	C	18

Similarly, the result of the formula `Table.Skip(TableC, each [Quantity]>10)` is shown in Table 8-42.

Table 8-42. *Result of Table.Skip*

Row	Date	Product Name	Quantity
3	2/1/2023	C	10
4	2/1/2023	A	1
5	2/1/2023	B	6
6	2/2/2023	B	9
7	2/2/2023	A	6
8	2/3/2023	C	6
9	2/4/2023	B	10
10	2/4/2023	A	3
11	2/6/2023	C	18

Table.RemoveRows

To delete n rows from the middle of a table, `Table.RemoveRows` can be used as follows:

```
Table.RemoveRows(
        table as table,
        offset as number,
        optional count as nullable number
            ) as table
```

This function takes three inputs.

1. The reference table is entered in the first input.

2. The starting point for deleting rows is determined in the second input. For example, entering the number 3 in this input means that row deletion starts from the fourth row.

3. The number of rows you want to delete is specified in this input.

Therefore, the result of Table.RemoveRows(TableC,3,5) is the modified version of TableC, in which rows from the fourth to the eighth (inclusive) have been removed. See Table 8-43.

Table 8-43. *Result of Table.RemoveRows*

Row	Date	Product Name	Quantity
1	1/30/2023	A	17
2	1/31/2023	A	18
3	2/1/2023	C	10
9	2/4/2023	B	10
10	2/4/2023	A	3
11	2/6/2023	C	18

Table.AlternateRows

Using Table.AlternateRows, a certain number of rows in a table can be removed based on a specific pattern, as follows:

```
Table.AlternateRows(
      table as table,
      offset as number,
      skip as number,
      take as number
         ) as table
```

The result of this function is always a table that includes several rows from the reference table. This function receives four inputs.

1. In the first input, the reference table is entered.

2. In this input, a number is entered that indicates the starting point for removing rows. In other words, entering 3 in this input means the first three rows of the table will be ignored and the deletion of rows will start from the fourth row.

3. In this input, a number is entered that represents the number of rows you want to delete at each iteration.

4. In this input, a number is entered, and its value represents the number of rows to be kept in each iteration (after deleting the number entered in the third input), and then the deletion operation is performed again.

According to this explanation, the result of the formula `Table.AlternateRows(TableC,3,2,1)` is calculated as follows: In TableC, the first three rows are ignored, and the deletion starts from the fourth row. In each iteration, two rows are deleted, and the next row (one row) is kept. The result is shown in Table 8-44.

Table 8-44. *Result of Table.AlternateRows*

Row	Date	Product Name	Quantity
1	1/30/2023	A	17
2	1/31/2023	A	18
3	2/1/2023	C	10
6	2/2/2023	B	9
9	2/4/2023	B	10

In a similar example, in the formula `Table.AlternateRows` (`TableC,3,2,2`), the first three rows are ignored, and the deletion starts from the fourth row. In each step, two rows are deleted and then two rows are left. The result of this formula is shown in Table 8-45.

Table 8-45. *Result of Table.AlternateRows*

Row	Date	Product Name	Quantity
1	1/30/2023	A	17
2	1/31/2023	A	18
3	2/1/2023	C	10
6	2/2/2023	B	9
7	2/2/2023	A	6
10	2/4/2023	A	3
11	2/6/2023	C	18

Table.RemoveRowsWithErrors

Table.RemoveRowsWithErrors is used to remove rows that have an error value in one of their columns, as follows:

```
Table.RemoveRowsWithErrors(
        table as table,
        optional columns as nullable list
        ) as table
```

This function takes two inputs.

1. The first input is the reference table.

2. The second input is the list of column titles. This input is optional; if no value is entered, all columns of the table will be considered in the evaluation.

If an error value occurs in any of the columns, the corresponding row will be deleted. However, if a list of column titles is entered in this input, only rows with an error value in one of the entered columns will be removed.

Table.RemoveMatchingRows

To remove rows with specific conditions from a table, Table. RemoveMatchingRows can be used as follows:

```
Table.RemoveMatchingRows(
        table as table,
        rows as list,
        optional equationCriteria as any
              ) as table
```

This function receives three inputs.

1.   The first input defines the reference table.

2.   The second input is defined as a list, including several records, and each record defines the condition for removing rows. For example, entering {[a=1]} means the rows with the value of 1 in column a should be deleted, and entering {[a=1],[a=2,b=1]} for this input means that rows with the value of 1 in column a should be deleted, but if the value of 2 is entered in column a, that row will be deleted only if the value of column b in that row is equal to 2.

3.   This input is optional and allows the user to specify custom criteria for comparing the values.

Considering the function explanation and TableC, the results of this function for different formulas are shown in Tables 8-46 through 8-48.

```
= Table.RemoveMatchingRows(TableC,{[Product
Name="A"]},"Product Name")
```

Table 8-46. *Result of Table.RemoveMatchingRows*

Row	Date	Product Name	Quantity
3	2/1/2023	C	10
5	2/1/2023	B	6
6	2/2/2023	B	9
8	2/3/2023	C	6
9	2/4/2023	B	10
11	2/6/2023	C	18

```
= Table.RemoveMatchingRows(
        TableC,
        {[Product Name="A"],[Product Name="B"]},
        "Product Name")
```

Table 8-47. *Result of Table.RemoveMatchingRows*

Row	Date	Product Name	Quantity
3	2/1/2023	C	10
8	2/3/2023	C	6
11	2/6/2023	C	18

```
= Table.RemoveMatchingRows(
      TableC,
      {[Product Name="A",Quantity=3]},
      {"Product Name","Quantity"})
```

Table 8-48. *Result of Table.RemoveMatchingRows*

Row	Date	Product Name	Quantity
1	1/30/2023	A	17
2	1/31/2023	A	18
3	2/1/2023	C	10
4	2/1/2023	A	1
5	2/1/2023	B	6
6	2/2/2023	B	9
7	2/2/2023	A	6
8	2/3/2023	C	6
9	2/4/2023	B	10
11	2/6/2023	C	18

Insert and Replace Table Rows

To insert new rows to a table, here are some functions

Table.InsertRows

Table.InsertRows is used to insert new rows between rows of a table:

```
Table.InsertRows(
        table as table,
        offset as number,
        rows as list
              ) as table
```

This function receives three inputs:

1. In the first input, the reference table is entered.

2. In this input, the position of adding new rows is determined by entering a specific number. For example, entering 3 in this input means that the new rows will be added after the fourth row in the reference table.

3. In the third input of this function, the new rows are defined as records which are inserted into a list.

Based on the function explanation, the result of the following formula is to add two new rows after the third row of the reference table:

```
= Table.InsertRows(TableC,3,
{[Row=12,Date="",Product Name="M",Quantity=7],
[Row=13,Date="",Product Name="M",Quantity=12]}
)
```

The result is shown in Table 8-49.

Table 8-49. *Result of Table.InsertRows*

Row	Date	Product Name	Quantity
1	1/30/2023	A	17
2	1/31/2023	A	18
3	2/1/2023	C	10
12		M	7
13		M	12
4	2/1/2023	A	1
5	2/1/2023	B	6
6	2/2/2023	B	9
7	2/2/2023	A	6
8	2/3/2023	C	6
9	2/4/2023	B	10
10	2/4/2023	A	3
11	2/6/2023	C	18

Table.ReplaceRows

Table.ReplaceRows is used to replace some rows of a table with new rows as follows:

```
Table.ReplaceRows(
    table as table,
    offset as number,
    count as number,
    rows as list
        ) as table
```

This function receives four inputs.

1. In the first input, the reference table is entered.

2. In the second input of this function, the starting point for deleting rows of the table is determined by entering a number. For example, entering the number 3 in this input means that the deletion operation starts from the fourth row of the reference table.

3. The third input of this function determines how many rows of the reference table should be deleted.

4. In this input, the new rows that you want to replace the deleted rows are entered. New rows are defined in the form of records entered in a list.

Based on the function explanation, the result of

```
= Table.ReplaceRows(TableC,3,5,
        {
         [Row=12,Date="",Product Name="M",Quantity=7],
         [Row=13,Date="",Product Name="M",Quantity=12]
        })
```

is as shown in Table 8-50.

Table 8-50. *Result of Table.InsertRows*

Row	Date	Product Name	Quantity
1	1/30/2023	A	17
2	1/31/2023	A	18
3	2/1/2023	C	10
12		M	7
13		M	12
9	2/4/2023	B	10
10	2/4/2023	A	3
11	2/6/2023	C	18

Table.ReplaceMatchingRows

Using `Table.ReplaceMatchingRows`, values entered in specific rows can be replaced with new values. This function is defined in Power Query as follows:

```
Table.ReplaceMatchingRows(
     table as table,
     replacements as list,
     optional equationCriteria as any
               ) as table
```

Based on the function syntax, it takes three inputs:

1. The first input defines the reference table.

2. The second input is a list containing pairs of values. The first value specifies the old value in the table as a record, and the second value specifies the replacement value as a record. For example, this

input can be entered as follows and means that if the value of column a is 1 and the value of column b is 2 at the same time, the value of column a will be changed to -1 and the value of column b will be changed to -2. And if the value of column a is -1 and the value of column b is 2 at the same time, the value of column a will be changed to -1.

```
{{[a=1,b=2],[a=-1,b=-2]},
{ [a=-1,b=2],[a=1,b=2]}}
```

3. The third input is optional and allows the user to specify custom criteria for comparing the values.

Table.Repeat

Using this function in Power Query, the rows of a table can be repeated as many times as determined in the second input of the function. Table.Repeat is defined in Power Query as follows:

```
Table.Repeat(
        table as table,
        count as number
        ) as table
```

According to the definition of this function, it receives two inputs:

1. The first input is the reference table.

2. The second input specifies how many times the rows of the table should be repeated. Entering the number 2 in this input means that all rows of the table should be repeated twice.

Therefore, the result of the formula Table.Repeat(TableC, 2) means all rows of TableC should be repeated twice. The result is shown in Table 8-51.

Table 8-51. *Result of Table.Repeat*

Row	Date	Product Name	Quantity
1	1/30/2023	A	17
2	1/31/2023	A	18
3	2/1/2023	C	10
4	2/1/2023	A	1
5	2/1/2023	B	6
6	2/2/2023	B	9
7	2/2/2023	A	6
8	2/3/2023	C	6
9	2/4/2023	B	10
10	2/4/2023	A	3
11	2/6/2023	C	18
1	1/30/2023	A	17
2	1/31/2023	A	18
3	2/1/2023	C	10
4	2/1/2023	A	1
5	2/1/2023	B	6
6	2/2/2023	B	9
7	2/2/2023	A	6
8	2/3/2023	C	6
9	2/4/2023	B	10
10	2/4/2023	A	3
11	2/6/2023	C	18

Order of rows

Functions can be used to change the order of the rows in a table.

Table.ReverseRows

Using `Table.ReverseRows`, the rows of a table can be reversed. This function is defined in Power Query as follows:

`Table.ReverseRows(`**`table`**` as table) as table`

`Table.ReverseRows` receives an input in the type of table and displays the reversed version of that table in the output. The result of `Table.ReverseRows(TableC)` is shown in Table 8-52.

Table 8-52. *Result of Table.ReverseRows*

Row	Date	Product Name	Quantity
11	2/6/2023	C	18
10	2/4/2023	A	3
9	2/4/2023	B	10
8	2/3/2023	C	6
7	2/2/2023	A	6
6	2/2/2023	B	9
5	2/1/2023	B	6
4	2/1/2023	A	1
3	2/1/2023	C	10
2	1/31/2023	A	18
1	1/30/2023	A	17

Table.Sort

To sort the rows of a table by specific logic such as ascending and descending, use Table.Sort as follows:

```
Table.Sort(
        table as table,
        comparisonCriteria as any
        ) as table
```

Based on the function syntax, it takes two nputs:

1. In the first input, the reference table is entered.

2. In the second input, the column name and logic for sorting are entered. To sort based on a single column, the column's name can be entered directly in double quotes (such as "Quantity"). It should be noted that the default sorting mode for values is ascending, but to change the sorting logic, instead of entering the column name in double quotes in this input, the column name and sorting logic should be entered inside a list such as {"Quantity", Order. Descending}. Additionally, to sort by more than one column, like ("Quantity", "Product Name"), the column names and the logic for sorting should be entered in separate lists such as

   ```
   {{"Quantity", Order.Descending},{"Product
   Name", Order.Descending}}
   ```

According to the function explanation, the result of the following formula is equal to the table sorted based on the Quantity column and is shown in Table 8-53.

```
= Table.Sort(TableC,"Quantity")
```

Table 8-53. *Result of Table.Sort*

Row	Date	Product Name	Quantity
4	2/1/2023	A	1
10	2/4/2023	A	3
7	2/2/2023	A	6
5	2/1/2023	B	6
8	2/3/2023	C	6
6	2/2/2023	B	9
3	2/1/2023	C	10
9	2/4/2023	B	10
1	1/30/2023	A	17
11	2/6/2023	C	18
2	1/31/2023	A	18

In the following formula, in addition to the Quantity column, the ProductName column has also been considered for sorting. See Table 8-54.

```
= Table.Sort(TableC,{"Quantity","Product Name"})
```

Table 8-54. *Result of Table.Sort*

Row	Date	Product Name	Quantity
4	2/1/2023	A	1
10	2/4/2023	A	3
7	2/2/2023	A	6
5	2/1/2023	B	6
8	2/3/2023	C	6
6	2/2/2023	B	9
9	2/4/2023	B	10
3	2/1/2023	C	10
1	1/30/2023	A	17
2	1/31/2023	A	18
11	2/6/2023	C	18

In the following formula, the basis for sorting the Quantity column is from largest to smallest, and in case of equal Quantity, the basis is the Product Name. See Table 8-55.

```
= Table.Sort(TableC,{{"Quantity",Order.
Descending},"Product Name"})
```

Table 8-55. *Result of Table.Sort*

Row	Date	Product Name	Quantity
2	1/31/2023	A	18
11	2/6/2023	C	18
1	1/30/2023	A	17
9	2/4/2023	B	10
3	2/1/2023	C	10
6	2/2/2023	B	9
7	2/2/2023	A	6
5	2/1/2023	B	6
8	2/3/2023	C	6
10	2/4/2023	A	3
4	2/1/2023	A	1

Checking a Condition in All Rows

There are several functions in Power Query for the evaluation of condition in the columns of a table.

Table.IsDistinct

To check the existence of duplicate rows in a table, `Table.IsDistinct` can be used as follows:

```
Table.IsDistinct(
        table as table,
        optional comparisonCriteria as any
                ) as logical
```

This function takes two inputs. If there are duplicate rows in the reference table based on determined columns in the second input, the result is false; in other cases, the result is true.

1. The reference table is entered in the first input.

2. This input is optional, and it defines the criteria for comparing values. For example, entering columns name in a list means searching for duplicate rows on the mentioned columns.

Considering TableC, the result of this function in different formulas is as follows.

The result of the following formula is True because there are no two rows in TableC that have the same data in all their columns:

```
= Table.IsDistinct(TableC)
```

However, if you define this function as follows, the result is False because the Product Name column has repeated names:

```
= Table.IsDistinct(TableC,"Product Name")
```

But if you also consider the date in comparison with the following formula, the result of the formula is True:

```
= Table.IsDistinct(TableC,{"Date","Product Name"})
```

Table.MatchesAllRows

Using Table.MatchesAllRows, a condition can be checked for all rows of a table. The result of the function is true if the defined condition is true for all rows, and false if the defined condition is not true for at least one row. This function is defined in Power Query as follows:

```
Table.MatchesAllRows(
        table as table,
        condition as function
              ) as logical
```

Based on the function syntax, it takes two inputs:

1. The first input is the reference table.

2. The second input specifies the desired condition.

So, the result of the following formula is true because all data in the Quantity column is positive:

```
= Table.MatchesAllRows(TableC,each [Quantity]>0)
```

Similarly, the result of the following formula is true because in the Product Name column, one of the three states "A", "B", and "C" exists:

```
= Table.MatchesAllRows(
TableC,
each [Product Name]="A" or [Product Name]="B" or [Product
Name]="C")
```

And since none of the product names are equal to X, the result of the following formula is also true:

```
= Table.MatchesAllRows(TableC,each [Product Name]<>"X")
```

However, the results of the following formulas are false:

```
= Table.MatchesAllRows(TableC,each [Product Name]="A")
= Table.MatchesAllRows(TableC,each [Quantity]>10)
= Table.MatchesAllRows(TableC,each Number.Mod([Quantity],2)=0)
```

Table.MatchesAnyRows

Table.MatchesAnyRows is like the Table.MatchesAllRows function, with the difference that the result of this function is true only if at least the defined conditions is true in one row of the table. The syntax of Table.MatchesAnyRows is as follows:

```
Table.MatchesAnyRows(
        table as table,
        condition as function
            ) as logical
```

This function takes two inputs:

1. The reference table is entered in the first input.

2. The desired condition is defined in the second input.

Based on the function explanation, the result of the following formula is True because at least in one row of the TableC, the product name is registered as A.

```
= Table.MatchesAnyRows(

TableC,

each [Product Name]="A")
```

Similarly, the result of the following formula is True because at least in one row of the table, the entered value in the Quantity column is equal to 10:

```
= Table.MatchesAnyRows(
        TableC,
        each [Quantity]=10)
```

The result of the following formula is True because in one row of the table, product A has been sold in the amount of 6:

```
= Table.MatchesAnyRows(
        TableC,
        each [Product Name]="A" and [Quantity]=6)
```

But the result of the following formula is false because in none of the rows of the table has product A been sold in the amount of 10 units:

```
= Table.MatchesAnyRows(
        TableC,
        each [Product Name]="A" and [Quantity]=10)
```

And, since the column of Product Name does not include the value of x, the result of the following formula is false:

```
= Table.MatchesAnyRows(
        TableC,
        each [Product Name]="X")
```

Table.Contains

To check the availability of a value in a table, Table.Contains can be used as follows:

```
Table.Contains(
        table as table,
        row as record,
        optional equationCriteria as any
              ) as logical
```

This function receives three inputs.

1. The first input is the reference table.

2. In the second input, the value that you are searching for and the column name for searching are determined as a record.

3. This input is optional and allows the user to specify custom criteria for comparing the values.

By considering the above description, the result of the following formula is True because the value 18 has been entered for the Quantity column in at least one of the rows in TableC:

```
= Table.Contains(
        TableC,
         [Quantity=18])
```

And the result of the following formula is False because there is no row in the table in which the product name is registered as B in the Product Name column with a Quantity value of 18:

```
= Table.Contains(
        TableC,
         [Product Name="B", Quantity=18])
```

But if the value "Quantity" is registered in the third input, it means that only the Quantity column is placed in the baseline comparison, so the result of the following formula is True:

```
= Table.Contains(
        TableC,
         [Product Name="B",Quantity=18],
         "Quantity")
```

Table.ContainsAll and Table.ContainsAny

These functions are like `Table.Contains`, except that in the `Table.`
`ContainsAll` and `Table.ContainsAny` functions, the existence of two or
more values on a column simultaneously can be checked. These functions
are defined in Power Query as follows, and the result of the `Table.`
`ContainsAll` function is True only if all the values specified in the second
input exist in the reference table, but in the `Table.ContainsAny` function,
if only one of the values exists in the reference table, the result of the
function is True.

```
Table.ContainsAll(
        table as table,
        rows as list,
        optional equationCriteria as any
            ) as logical
```

```
Table.ContainsAny(
        table as table,
        rows as list,
        optional equationCriteria as any
            ) as logical
```

Both functions takes three inputs.

1. In the first input, the reference table is defined.

2. In this input, a list of values that you want to
   check the existence of in the columns is entered.
   The values should be entered in separate records
   within a list.

3. This input is optional and allows you to specify
   custom criteria for comparing the values.

Considering TableC, the result of the following formula is True because the numbers 18 and 10 are registered in the Quantity column of the reference table:

```
= Table.ContainsAll(
        TableC,
        {[Quantity=18],[Quantity=10]})
```

But since the Quantity column in the reference table does not include the 12, the result of the following formula is False:

```
= Table.ContainsAll(
        TableC,
        {[Quantity=18],[Quantity=10],[Quantity=12]})
```

By using `Table.ContainsAny` instead of `Table.ContainsAll` in the above formula, since at least one of the values 18, 10, or 12 is registered in the Quantity column in the reference table, the result is True. Therefore, the result of the following formula is True:

```
= Table.ContainsAny(
        TableC,
        {[Quantity=18],[Quantity=10],[Quantity=12]})
```

Table.SingleRow

`Table.SingleRow` receives an input in the format of the table, and if that table has only one row, this function displays the result of that row as a record in the output; otherwise, the result of this function is an error. This function is defined in Power Query as follows:

```
Table.SingleRow(table as table) as record
```

245

Column Names

To extract the list of column names and change them, there are different functions that are discussed in this section. To simplify the example, TableC is used in different formulas.

Table.ColumnNames

By using this function with the following syntax, the column's names of a table can be extracted:

```
Table.ColumnNames(table as table) as list
```

This function takes a table as input and displays its column titles as a list in the output. Therefore, the result of the formula `Table.ColumnNames(TableC)` is equal to this list:

```
{"Row","Date","Product Name","Quantity"}
```

Table.DemoteHeaders

If the first row of a table has been mistakenly identified as column headers, `Table.DemoteHeaders` can be used to return the column headers to the first row of the table. This function takes a table as input, then adds the column headers of the table as the first row, and names the table's columns as Column1, Column2, and so on.

```
Table.DemoteHeaders(table as table) as table
```

So, the result of the formula `Table.DemoteHeaders(TableC)` is as shown in Table 8-56.

Table 8-56. *Result of Table.DemoteHeaders(TableC)*

Column1	Column2	Column3	Column4
Row	Date	Product Name	Quantity
1	1/30/2023	A	17
2	1/31/2023	A	18
3	2/1/2023	C	10
4	2/1/2023	A	1
5	2/1/2023	B	6
6	2/2/2023	B	9
7	2/2/2023	A	6
8	2/3/2023	C	6
9	2/4/2023	B	10
10	2/4/2023	A	3
11	2/6/2023	C	18

Table.PromoteHeaders

Using Table.PromoteHeaders, the values entered in the first row of the table are promoted to the header. This function is defined in Power Query as follows:

```
Table.PromoteHeaders(
        table as table,
        optional options as nullable record
                ) as table
```

This function receives two inputs.

1. The first input is the reference table.

2. The second input is used to add values with the date
    or time format as a header. In the default mode,
    only the values in text and number format can be
    used for the column titles; values with the date or
    time format cannot be used for the column title. To
    solve this problem, entering [PromoteAllScalars
    = true, Culture = "en-US"] in this input makes
    it possible to register dates in the header column
    as well.

Therefore, the result of = Table.PromoteHeaders(TableC) is as
Table 8-57.

Table 8-57. *Result of Table.PromoteHeaders(TableC)*

1	Column2	A	17
2	1/31/2023	A	18
3	2/1/2023	C	10
4	2/1/2023	A	1
5	2/1/2023	B	6
6	2/2/2023	B	9
7	2/2/2023	A	6
8	2/3/2023	C	6
9	2/4/2023	B	10
10	2/4/2023	A	3
11	2/6/2023	C	18

And the result of the following formula is in Table 8-58:

```
= Table.PromoteHeaders(TableC,   [PromoteAllScalars = true,
Culture = "en-US"])
```

Table 8-58. *Result of Table.PromoteHeaders*

1	1/30/2023	A	17
2	1/31/2023	A	18
3	2/1/2023	C	10
4	2/1/2023	A	1
5	2/1/2023	B	6
6	2/2/2023	B	9
7	2/2/2023	A	6
8	2/3/2023	C	6
9	2/4/2023	B	10
10	2/4/2023	A	3
11	2/6/2023	C	18

Table.HasColumns

To evaluate the existence of one or more columns (based on the column titles) within a table, Table.HasColumns can be used as follows:

```
Table.HasColumns(
        table as table,
        columns as any
            ) as logical
```

This function receives two inputs.

1. In the first input, the reference table is entered.

2. The names of the columns that you are searching for in the reference table are inserted in a text or list in this input.

The applications of this function are given in Table 8-59.

Table 8-59. *Result of Table.HasColumns*

Formula	Result
= Table.HasColumns(TableC,"Product Name")	True
= Table.HasColumns(TableC,"Tax")	False
= Table.HasColumns(TableC,{"Product Name","Quantity"})	True

Table.ColumnsOfType

To extract column name with specific format of values, `Table.ColumnsOfType` can be used as follows:

`Table.ColumnsOfType(`**table** `as table,` **listOfTypes** `as list) as list`

Based on the function syntax, it receives two inputs.

1. The first input defines the reference table.

2. The second input defines the desired values formats as a list.

The output of this function is a list that includes the titles of the table columns with the searching format. Therefore, according to the above explanation, the result of the following formula is equal to all the column names with the value format of any, so it is equal to {"Row", "Date", "Product Name", "Quantity"}:

```
= Table.ColumnsOfType(TableC,{type any})
```

Table.PrefixColumns

This function is used in Power Query to add a prefix before the name of all columns as follows:

```
Table.PrefixColumns(
        table as table,
        prefix as text
            ) as table
```

Table.PrefixColumns takes two arguments.

1. The first argument is the reference table.

2. The prefix is entered in the second argument in the text format.

The output of this function is a table like the reference table, except that a prefix has been added before the title of all columns.

For example, the result of the formula = Table.PrefixColumns(TableC,"New") is shown in Table 8-60.

Table 8-60. *Result of Table.PrefixColumns*

New.Row	New.Date	New.Product Name	New.Quantity
1	1/30/2023	A	17
2	1/31/2023	A	18
3	2/1/2023	C	10
4	2/1/2023	A	1
5	2/1/2023	B	6
6	2/2/2023	B	9
7	2/2/2023	A	6
8	2/3/2023	C	6
9	2/4/2023	B	10
10	2/4/2023	A	3
11	2/6/2023	C	18

Table.RenameColumns

As the name of this function suggests, `Table.RenameColumns` is used to rename column titles in a table as follows:

```
Table.RenameColumns(
        table as table,
        renames as list,
        optional missingField as nullable number
            ) as table
```

Table.RenameColumns takes three inputs.

1. The first input is the reference table.

2. The second input of this function contains a list of old and new names. To rename a column, a list as {"new name", "old name"} can be entered in this input, but to rename more than one column, the corresponding list must be defined as {{"new name 2", "old name 2"}, {"new name 1", "old name 1"}}.

3. This input is optional, and it is applied if the reference table does not include a column with one of the names mentioned in the second input by entering MissingField.Error (or number 0), MissingField.Ignore (or number 1), and MissingField.UseNull (or number 2).

Consider the following formulas and the results (Tables 8-61 and 8-62:

= Table.RenameColumns(TableC,{"Product Name","P_Name"})

Table 8-61. *Result of Table.RenameColumns*

Row	Date	P_Name	Quantity
1	1/30/2023	A	17
2	1/31/2023	A	18
3	2/1/2023	C	10
4	2/1/2023	A	1
5	2/1/2023	B	6
6	2/2/2023	B	9
7	2/2/2023	A	6
8	2/3/2023	C	6
9	2/4/2023	B	10
10	2/4/2023	A	3
11	2/6/2023	C	18

```
= Table.RenameColumns(
      TableC,
      {{"Product Name","P_Name"},{"Quantity","Amount"}})
```

Table 8-62. *Result of Table.RenameColumns*

Row	Date	P_Name	Amount
1	1/30/2023	A	17
2	1/31/2023	A	18
3	2/1/2023	C	10
4	2/1/2023	A	1
5	2/1/2023	B	6
6	2/2/2023	B	9
7	2/2/2023	A	6
8	2/3/2023	C	6
9	2/4/2023	B	10
10	2/4/2023	A	3
11	2/6/2023	C	18

Modifing columns

There are several functions in the Power Query for modifying columns by adding, removing, or reordering columns and they are described in this section. To simplify the examples, TableC is used in the examples of this part.

Table.RemoveColumns

Using Table.RemoveColumns, extra columns in a table can be removed as follows:

```
Table.RemoveColumns(
        table as table,
        columns as any,
        optional missingField as nullable number
            ) as table
```

This function receives three inputs.

1. The first input specifies the reference table.

2. The name of columns that should be deleted are determined in this input. To remove one column, its name can directly insert as text in this input, but to remove more than one column, their names can be entered inside a list.

3. This input is optional and is applied to the case when the reference table does not contain the column with the name mentioned in the second input. Three different values of MissingField.Error (or number 0), MissingField.Ignore (or number 1), and MissingField.UseNull (or number 2) can be used in this input.

Based on this explanation, the result of = Table.RemoveColumns(TableC, "Row") is equal to Table 8-63.

Table 8-63. *Result of Table.RemoveColumns*

Date	Product Name	Quantity
1/30/2023	A	17
1/31/2023	A	18
2/1/2023	C	10
2/1/2023	A	1
2/1/2023	B	6
2/2/2023	B	9
2/2/2023	A	6
2/3/2023	C	6
2/4/2023	B	10
2/4/2023	A	3
2/6/2023	C	18

The result of the following formula is equal to Table 8-64.

```
= Table.RemoveColumns(
        TableC,
        {"Row","Quantity"})
```

Table 8-64. *Result of Table.RemoveColumns*

Date	Product Name
1/30/2023	A
1/31/2023	A
2/1/2023	C
2/1/2023	A
2/1/2023	B
2/2/2023	B
2/2/2023	A
2/3/2023	C
2/4/2023	B
2/4/2023	A
2/6/2023	C

In another case, if the name of a column is mistakenly entered in the second input (for example, instead of "Quantity", "Quantity2" is entered), the formula result is an error:

```
=Table.RemoveColumns(TableC,{"Row","Quantity2"})
```

In this case, the third input of this function can be used as follows:

```
=Table.RemoveColumns(
        TableC,
        {"Row","Quantity2"},
        MissingField.UseNull )
```

The result is as shown in Table 8-65.

Table 8-65. *Result of Table.RemoveColumns*

Date	Product Name	Quantity
1/30/2023	A	17
1/31/2023	A	18
2/1/2023	C	10
2/1/2023	A	1
2/1/2023	B	6
2/2/2023	B	9
2/2/2023	A	6
2/3/2023	C	6
2/4/2023	B	10
2/4/2023	A	3
2/6/2023	C	18

Table.SelectColumns

In order to remove most of columns in a table, instead of using Table.
RemoveColumn and mentioning the name of columns that you want to
remove, Table.SelectColumns with the following syntax can be used.
In this case, the name of columns that you want to present in the output
should be entered in the second inpuy.

```
Table.SelectColumns(
        table as table,
        columns as any,
        optional missingField as nullable number
                ) as table
```

This function receives three inputs.

1. In the first input, the reference table is entered.

2. In the second input, the name of the column(s)
    that you want to select is entered. To search for a
    column, its name is directly entered in this input,
    but to search for more than a column, their names
    should be entered in a list.

3. This input is optional and is used to set the settings
    for the case where the entered column names in
    the second input are not present in the column
    titles of the reference table. This input is optional
    and includes three states: `MissingField.Error` (or
    number 0), `MissingField.Ignore` (or number 1),
    and `MissingField.UseNull` (or number 2).

Based on the function explanation, the results of the different states of
this function are shown in Table 8-66:

```
= Table.SelectColumns(TableC,"Date")
```

Table 8-66. *Result of Table.SelectColumns*

Date
1/30/2023
1/31/2023
2/1/2023
2/1/2023
2/1/2023
2/2/2023
2/2/2023
2/3/2023
2/4/2023
2/4/2023
2/6/2023

The result of this formula is shown in Table 8-67:

```
= Table.SelectColumns(
        TableC,
        {"Product Name","Row","Quantity"})
```

Table 8-67. *Result of Table.SelectColumns*

Product Name	Row	Quantity
A	1	17
A	2	18
C	3	10
A	4	1
B	5	6
B	6	9
A	7	6
C	8	6
B	9	10
A	10	3
C	11	18

In another case, the result of the following formula is an error because the column named Quantity2 does not exist in the base table:

```
= Table.SelectColumns(
        TableC,
        {"Date","Quantity2"})
```

In this case, using the third input of this function as follows, the result of the function is as shown in Table 8-68 instead of an error:

```
= Table.SelectColumns(
        TableC,
        {"Date","Quantity2"},
        MissingField.Ignore)
```

Table 8-68. *Result of Table.SelectColumns*

Date
1/30/2023
1/31/2023
2/1/2023
2/1/2023
2/1/2023
2/2/2023
2/2/2023
2/3/2023
2/4/2023
2/4/2023
2/6/2023

Table.DuplicateColumn

By this function, a copy of the columns in the table can be created. The syntax of this function in Power Query is as follows:

```
Table.DuplicateColumn(
        table as table,
        columnName as text,
        newColumnName as text,
        optional columnType as nullable type
            ) as table
```

This function takes four inputs.

1. In the first input, the reference table is entered.

2. In the second input, it is determined which column should be duplicated by entering its name as a text value.

3. The name of the new column is determined in this input.

4. The format of values in the new column is specified in the fourth input by entering the format type after the word "type", such as "type text".

Based on the function explanation, using the following function, a copy of the Product Name column has been added to the table and its name has been defined in the new table as "Product Name 2", as you can see in Table 8-69.

```
= Table.DuplicateColumn(
        TableC,
        "Product Name",
        "Product Name 2")
```

Table 8-69. *Result of Table.DuplicateColumns*

Row	Date	Product Name	Quantity	Product Name 2
1	1/30/2023	A	17	A
2	1/31/2023	A	18	A
3	2/1/2023	C	10	C
4	2/1/2023	A	1	A
5	2/1/2023	B	6	B
6	2/2/2023	B	9	B
7	2/2/2023	A	6	A
8	2/3/2023	C	6	C
9	2/4/2023	B	10	B
10	2/4/2023	A	3	A
11	2/6/2023	C	18	C

Table.TransformColumnTypes

To change the format of values in the columns of a table, this function is used as follows:

```
Table.TransformColumnTypes(
        table as table,
        typeTransformations as list,
        optional culture as nullable text
        ) as table
```

Based on the function syntax, it takes three inputs:

1. In the first input, the reference table is entered.

2. The name of columns and their desired formats are entered in the lists with two values, and all the lists are entered in a list in this input. For example, {"A", type text} means that the format of the values in column A should be changed to text.

3. This input is optional and specifies the mode for changing the format.

Considering TableC, the following formula can be used to change the column formats:

```
= Table.TransformColumnTypes(
        TableC,
        {{"Row", Percentage.Type},
        {"Date", type datetime}})
```

The result of this function is the same as TableC in which the format of values in the Row column has been changed to percentage and the Date column has been changed to date and time. See Table 8-70.

Table 8-70. Result of Table.TransformColumnTypes

Row	Date	Product Name	Quantity
100.00%	1/30/2023 12:00:00 AM	A	17
200.00%	1/31/2023 12:00:00 AM	A	18
300.00%	2/1/2023 12:00:00 AM	C	10
400.00%	2/1/2023 12:00:00 AM	A	1
500.00%	2/1/2023 12:00:00 AM	B	6
600.00%	2/2/2023 12:00:00 AM	B	9
700.00%	2/2/2023 12:00:00 AM	A	6
800.00%	2/3/2023 12:00:00 AM	C	6
900.00%	2/4/2023 12:00:00 AM	B	10
1000.00%	2/4/2023 12:00:00 AM	A	3
1100.00%	2/6/2023 12:00:00 AM	C	18

Table.TransformColumns

To apply modifications (such as multiplying, adding a specific number to the column values, cleaning text values, or removing extra spaces) to the columns of a table, this function can be used as follows:

```
Table.TransformColumns(
        table as table,
        transformOperations as list,
        optional defaultTransformation as nullable function,
        optional missingField as nullable number
            ) as table
```

Based on the function syntax, it takes four inputs:

1. The reference table is entered in the first input.

2. In the second input, the column name and modification function are entered in a list. For example, {{"A",Text.From},{"B",Number.From}} means the values in column A should be changed to text format and the values in column B should be changed to numeric format.

3. The third input of this function is optional.

4. The fourth input of this function is optional and is used to specify the result of the function in case the reference table does not include the column name entered in the second input. The three options of MissingField.Error, MissingField.Ignore, and MissingField.UseNull can be used in this input, which mean respectively to show an error, the non-matching field should be ignored, or the results of that field should be displayed as Null.

Based on the function explanations and using TableC, the result of this function in different scenarios is explained.

In the following formula, the value of 2 should be added to the values in the Quantity column in TableC:

```
= Table.TransformColumns(
        TableC,
        {"Quantity",each _+2})
```

The result of this formula is shown in Table 8-71.

Table 8-71. *Result of Table.TransformColumns*

Row	Date	Product Name	Quantity
1	1/30/2023	A	19
2	1/31/2023	A	20
3	2/1/2023	C	12
4	2/1/2023	A	3
5	2/1/2023	B	8
6	2/2/2023	B	11
7	2/2/2023	A	8
8	2/3/2023	C	8
9	2/4/2023	B	12
10	2/4/2023	A	5
11	2/6/2023	C	20

In another example, the following formula states that the information in the Date column should be displayed as day, the word "Product" should be added in front of the product names, and the values in the Quantity column should be multiplied by 3:

```
= Table.TransformColumns(
      TableC,
      {{"Date",each Date.Day(_)},
      {"Product Name",each "Product: " & _},
      {"Quantity",each _+2}})
```

The results are shown in Table 8-72.

Table 8-72. *Result of Table.TransformColumns*

Row	Date	Product Name	Quantity
1	30	Product: A	19
2	31	Product: A	20
3	1	Product: C	12
4	1	Product: A	3
5	1	Product: B	8
6	2	Product: B	11
7	2	Product: A	8
8	3	Product: C	8
9	4	Product: B	12
10	4	Product: A	5
11	6	Product: C	20

In another example, instead of displaying the sales volume on the Quantity column, the share from the total sale is presented in the output using the following formula:

```
= Table.TransformColumns(
        TableC,
        {"Quantity",each _/List.Sum(TableC[Quantity]) }
        )
```

If this formula is used, the result is obtained in the form of Table 8-73.

Table 8-73. Result of Table.TransformColumns

Row	Date	Product Name	Quantity
1	1/30/2023	A	0.163461538
2	1/31/2023	A	0.173076923
3	2/1/2023	C	0.096153846
4	2/1/2023	A	0.009615385
5	2/1/2023	B	0.057692308
6	2/2/2023	B	0.086538462
7	2/2/2023	A	0.057692308
8	2/3/2023	C	0.057692308
9	2/4/2023	B	0.096153846
10	2/4/2023	A	0.028846154
11	2/6/2023	C	0.173076923

Table.AddIndexColumn

Table.AddIndexColumn can be used as follows to add a new index column
to the table:

```
Table.AddIndexColumn(
        table as table,
        newColumnName as text,
        optional initialValue as nullable number,
        optional increment as nullable number,
        optional columnType as nullable type
                ) as table
```

Based on the function syntax, it takes five inputs.

1. The first input specifies the reference table.

2. The name of the new column is entered as text in the second input.

3. This input is optional (its default value is 0) and specifies the starting number for numbering the new column.

4. This input is optional (its default value is 1) and specifies the increment or decrement of values in the new column in comparison to the previous row.

5. This input is optional and specifies the format of values in the new column.

Based on the above explanation, the result of the following formula is shown in Table 8-74:

```
= Table.AddIndexColumn(TableC,"Index Column")
```

Table 8-74. *Result of Table.AddIndexColumn*

Row	Date	Product Name	Quantity	Index Column
1	1/30/2023	A	17	0
2	1/31/2023	A	18	1
3	2/1/2023	C	10	2
4	2/1/2023	A	1	3
5	2/1/2023	B	6	4
6	2/2/2023	B	9	5
7	2/2/2023	A	6	6
8	2/3/2023	C	6	7
9	2/4/2023	B	10	8
10	2/4/2023	A	3	9
11	2/6/2023	C	18	10

And in a similar example, the result of the following formula is equal to a new column whose values start from 4 and decrease by 2 in each row. See Table 8-75.

```
= Table.AddIndexColumn(
        TableC,
        "Index Column",
        4,
        -2)
```

Table 8-75. Result of Table.AddIndexColumn

Row	Date	Product Name	Quantity	Index Column
1	1/30/2023	A	17	4
2	1/31/2023	A	18	2
3	2/1/2023	C	10	0
4	2/1/2023	A	1	-2
5	2/1/2023	B	6	-4
6	2/2/2023	B	9	-6
7	2/2/2023	A	6	-8
8	2/3/2023	C	6	-10
9	2/4/2023	B	10	-12
10	2/4/2023	A	3	-14
11	2/6/2023	C	18	-16

Table.AddColumn

The `Table.AddColumn` function is one of the most important functions in Power Query and is used to add a new column to a table as follows:

```
Table.AddColumn(
        table as table,
        newColumnName as text,
        columnGenerator as function,
        optional columnType as nullable type
            ) as table
```

Based on the function syntax, it takes four inputs.

1. The reference table is entered in the first input.

2. In the second input, the title of the new column is specified as a text value.

3. In the third input, the formula for calculating values in the new column is determined. In this input, other columns can be referred to by mentioning their name between [ ].

4. The fourth input is optional and can be used to specify the format of values in the new column.

For example, in this formula, a new column is added to the TableC that specifies the year for each row. See Table 8-76.

```
= Table.AddColumn(TableC,"Year",each Date.Year([Date]))
```

Table 8-76. *Result of Table.AddColumn*

Row	Date	Product Name	Quantity	Year
1	1/30/2023	A	17	2023
2	1/31/2023	A	18	2023
3	2/1/2023	C	10	2023
4	2/1/2023	A	1	2023
5	2/1/2023	B	6	2023
6	2/2/2023	B	9	2023
7	2/2/2023	A	6	2023
8	2/3/2023	C	6	2023
9	2/4/2023	B	10	2023
10	2/4/2023	A	3	2023
11	2/6/2023	C	18	2023

In the following example, the month name for each row is added to the table. See Table 8-77.

```
= Table.AddColumn(
        TableC,
        "Month",
        each Date.MonthName([Date]))
```

Table 8-77. *Result of Table.AddColumn*

Row	Date	Product Name	Quantity	Month
1	1/30/2023	A	17	January
2	1/31/2023	A	18	January
3	2/1/2023	C	10	February
4	2/1/2023	A	1	February
5	2/1/2023	B	6	February
6	2/2/2023	B	9	February
7	2/2/2023	A	6	February
8	2/3/2023	C	6	February
9	2/4/2023	B	10	February
10	2/4/2023	A	3	February
11	2/6/2023	C	18	February

In the following example, by examining the value of the Quantity column, it is determined which of the rows in the table contain a number greater than 10. The formula adds a new column called "Greater than 10" to TableC and uses the "each [Quantity]>10" function to check if the quantity value in each row is greater than 10 (Table 8-78).

Table 8-78. *Result of Table.AddColumn*

Row	Date	Product Name	Quantity	Greater than 10
1	1/30/2023	A	17	TRUE
2	1/31/2023	A	18	TRUE
3	2/1/2023	C	10	FALSE
4	2/1/2023	A	1	FALSE
5	2/1/2023	B	6	FALSE
6	2/2/2023	B	9	FALSE
7	2/2/2023	A	6	FALSE
8	2/3/2023	C	6	FALSE
9	2/4/2023	B	10	FALSE
10	2/4/2023	A	3	FALSE
11	2/6/2023	C	18	TRUE

Table.AddRankColumn

Using Table.AddRankColumn, the rows of a table can be ranked based on their values as follows:

```
Table.AddRankColumn(
        table as table,
        newColumnName as text,
        comparisonCriteria as any,
        optional options as nullable record
                ) as table
```

Based on the function syntax, it takes four inputs.

1. In the first input, the reference table is entered.

2. The title of the new column is determined in the second input.

3. The comparison criterion of the rows is specified in this input. In the simplest case, in this input, the title of a column can be entered textually as the ranking criterion.

4. The fourth input of this function represents the settings related to ranking. This input is optional and you can use the following options: RankKind. Competition (equivalent to the number 0), RankKind.Dense (equivalent to the number 1), and RankKind.Ordinal (equivalent to the number 2). RankKind.Competition is the default value and determines that rows with the same value receive the same rank and a gap is created between their rank and the rank of next value (for example, there are two rows with rank 1 and the next row has rank 3, and there is no row with rank 2). In RankKind. Dense, rows with the same value receive the same rank, and there is no gap between their rank and the rank of next value (for example, two rows with rank 1 are created and the rank of the next row is 2). In the RankKind.Ordinal state, all rows (even those with the same value) receive a unique rank.

According to the function explanation, the result of the following formula is equal to Table 8-79:

```
= Table.AddRankColumn(
        TableC,
        "rank",
        "Quantity")
```

Table 8-79. *Result of Table.AddRankColumn*

Row	Date	Product Name	Quantity	rank
4	2/1/2023	A	1	1
10	2/4/2023	A	3	2
5	2/1/2023	B	6	3
7	2/2/2023	A	6	3
8	2/3/2023	C	6	3
6	2/2/2023	B	9	6
3	2/1/2023	C	10	7
9	2/4/2023	B	10	7
1	1/30/2023	A	17	9
2	1/31/2023	A	18	10
11	2/6/2023	C	18	10

In another case, the result of the following formula is equal to a ranked table with the difference that rows receive higher rankings based on their higher sales, as shown in Table 8-80.

```
= Table.AddRankColumn(
        TableC,
        "rank"
        ,{"Quantity",Order.Descending})
```

Table 8-80. *Result of Table.AddRankColumn*

Row	Date	Product Name	Quantity	rank
2	1/31/2023	A	18	1
11	2/6/2023	C	18	1
1	1/30/2023	A	17	3
3	2/1/2023	C	10	4
9	2/4/2023	B	10	4
6	2/2/2023	B	9	6
5	2/1/2023	B	6	7
7	2/2/2023	A	6	7
8	2/3/2023	C	6	7
10	2/4/2023	A	3	10
4	2/1/2023	A	1	11

In another situation, if you want to change the logic of ranking, you can use the following formula:

```
= Table.AddRankColumn(
        TableC,
        "rank",
        {"Quantity",Order.Descending},
        [RankKind =RankKind.Dense])
```

In this situation, the result is obtained in the form of Table 8-81.

Table 8-81. *Result of Table.AddRank*

Row	Date	Product Name	Quantity	rank
2	1/31/2023	A	18	1
11	2/6/2023	C	18	1
1	1/30/2023	A	17	2
3	2/1/2023	C	10	3
9	2/4/2023	B	10	3
6	2/2/2023	B	9	4
5	2/1/2023	B	6	5
7	2/2/2023	A	6	5
8	2/3/2023	C	6	5
10	2/4/2023	A	3	6
4	2/1/2023	A	1	7

Table.SplitColumn

Table.SplitColumn can be used to divide the values in a column of a table into multiple columns based on a specific criterion. This function is defined in Power Query as follows:

```
Table.SplitColumn(
        table as table,
        sourceColumn as text,
        splitter as function,
        optional columnNamesOrNumber as any,
        optional default as any,
        optional extraColumns as any
            ) as table
```

Based on the function syntax, it takes six inputs.

1. The first input is the reference table.

2. The second input is the name of the column that you want to divide into multiple columns.

3. The splitter function is entered as the third input. In this input, one of the following functions can be used:

```
Splitter.SplitByNothing
Splitter.SplitTextByCharacterTransition
Splitter.SplitTextByAnyDelimiter
Splitter.SplitTextByDelimiter
Splitter.SplitTextByEachDelimiter
Splitter.SplitTextByLengths
Splitter.SplitTextByPositions
Splitter.SplitTextByRanges
Splitter.SplitTextByRepeatedLengths
Splitter.SplitTextByWhitespace
```

4. The names or numbers of the new columns are specified in the fourth input of this function.

5. The fifth input of this function is optional and determines the default value of the function. In the normal state, the default value of the function is null. After separating, null is presented in the columns with no value. While using this input, instead of the word null, another word can be shown.

6. The sixth input of this function is also optional.

Based on the above explanation, considering TableC and assuming that the information in the date column is in text format, this formula indicates that the information in the date column should be divided into multiple columns based on the "/" and displayed in three columns named Date.1, Date.2, and Date.3:

```
= Table.SplitColumn(
        TableC,
        "Date",
        Splitter.SplitTextByDelimiter("/"),
        {"Date.1", "Date.2", "Date.3"})
```

Therefore, the result of this formula is equal to Table 8-82.

Table 8-82. *Result of Table.SplitColumn*

Row	Date.1	Date.2	Date.3	Product Name	Quantity
1	1	30	2023	A	17
2	1	31	2023	A	18
3	2	1	2023	C	10
4	2	1	2023	A	1
5	2	1	2023	B	6
6	2	2	2023	B	9
7	2	2	2023	A	6
8	2	3	2023	C	6
9	2	4	2023	B	10
10	2	4	2023	A	3
11	2	6	2023	C	18

It is possible to change the column names and use two similar columns instead of three with the following formula:

```
= Table.SplitColumn(
        TableC,
        "Date",
        Splitter.SplitTextByDelimiter("/"),
        {"Day", "Month"})
```

The result of this function is shown in Table 8-83.

Table 8-83. *Result of Table.SplitColumn*

Row	Day	Month	Product Name	Quantity
1	1	30	A	17
2	1	31	A	18
3	2	1	C	10
4	2	1	A	1
5	2	1	B	6
6	2	2	B	9
7	2	2	A	6
8	2	3	C	6
9	2	4	B	10
10	2	4	A	3
11	2	6	C	18

The following formula specifies that the information in this column should be separated into three separate columns, each consisting of three characters:

```
= Table.SplitColumn(
        TableC,
        "Date",
        Splitter.SplitTextByRepeatedLengths(3),
        {"Date.1", "Date.2", "Date.3"})
```

The result of this function is shown in Table 8-84.

Table 8-84. *Result of Table.SplitColumn*

Row	Date.1	Date.2	Date.3	Product Name	Quantity
1	1/3	0/2	023	A	17
2	1/3	1/2	023	A	18
3	2/1	/20	23	C	10
4	2/1	/20	23	A	1
5	2/1	/20	23	B	6
6	2/2	/20	23	B	9
7	2/2	/20	23	A	6
8	2/3	/20	23	C	6
9	2/4	/20	23	B	10
10	2/4	/20	23	A	3
11	2/6	/20	23	C	18

Table.CombineColumns

Using Table.CombineColumns, the values of two or more columns can be merged into a new column. This function is defined in Power Query as follows:

```
Table.CombineColumns(
     table as table,
     sourceColumns as list,
     combiner as function,
     column as text
          ) as table
```

This function receives four inputs.

1. The name of the reference table is entered in this input.

2. In this input, a list of column names that you want to merge together is entered.

3. In this input, the column combination function is determined by entering one of the following values:

   ```
   Combiner.CombineTextByDelimiter
   Combiner.CombineTextByEachDelimiter
   Combiner.CombineTextByLengths
   Combiner.CombineTextByPositions
   Combiner.CombineTextByRanges
   ```

4. In the last input of this function, the name of the new column is entered as a text value.

To examine this function, consider Table 8-85 named TableG.

Table 8-85. *Definition of TableG*

Name	Family	Age
Sara	Sani	18
Omid	Motamedi	32
Mohamad	Abed	26

In this case, the result of

```
= Table.CombineColumns(
        TableG,
        {"Name", "Family"},
        Combiner.CombineTextByDelimiter(","),
        "New Column")
```

is equal to Table 8-86, in which the name and family are placed next to each other and separated by a comma.

Table 8-86. *Result of Table.CombineColumns*

New Column	Age
Sara, Sani	18
Omid, Motamedi	32
Mohamad, Abed	26

If the following formula is used, the first three characters of the name and the first two characters of the family will be placed next to each other:

```
= Table.CombineColumns(
        TableG,
        {"Name", "Family"},
        Combiner.CombineTextByLengths({3,2}),
        "New Column")
```

The result of this formula is as shown in Table 8-87.

Table 8-87. *Result of Table.CombineColumns*

New Column	Age
SarSa	18
OmiMo	32
MohAb	26

Table.CombineColumnsToRecord

Table.CombineColumnsToRecord is used to combine values from two or more columns into a record and display them in one column in Power Query as follows:

```
Table.CombineColumnsToRecord(
        table as table,
        newColumnName as text,
        sourceColumns as list,
        optional options as nullable record
                        ) as table
```

This function receives four inputs.

1. The reference table is entered in the first input.

2. The name of the new column is specified as a text value in the second input of the function.

3. The list of column names that you want to merge is defined in the third input of the function.

4. This input is optional and contains settings related to the merger.

To evaluate the result of this function, consider TableK as shown in Table 8-88.

Table 8-88. *Definition of TableK*

New Column	Age
Sara, Sani	18
Omid, Motamedi	32
Mohamad, Abed	26

The result of

```
= Table.CombineColumnsToRecord(
        TableK,
        "New Column",
        {"Name", "Family"})
```

is shown in Table 8-89.

Table 8-89. *Result of Table.CombineColumnsToRecord*

New Column	Age
[Record]	18
[Record]	32
[Record]	26

In this output, each of the values in the New Column is a record that includes the name and surname.

Table.ReorderColumns

To change the order of columns in a table, `Table.ReorderColumns` can be used as follows:

```
Table.ReorderColumns(
        table as table,
        columnOrder as list,
        optional missingField as nullable number
                    ) as table
```

The output of this function is the same as the input table, except that the order of columns in the output table has changed. This function receives three inputs:

1. The first input of this function specifies the reference table.

2. The second input is a list that includes the names of columns in the desired order.

3. This input is optional and determines the logic of calculation if the reference table does not contain columns with the name equal to what is entered in the second input. `MissingField.Error` (or number 0), `MissingField.Ignore` (or number 1), and `MissingField.UseNull` (or number 2) can be used in this input.

Based on the function explanation, the result of the following formula is shown in Table 8-90:

```
= Table.ReorderColumns(TableC,{"Product Name","Row","Quantity","Date"})
```

Table 8-90. *Result of Table.ReorderColumns*

Product Name	Row	Quantity	Date
A	1	17	1/30/2023
A	2	18	1/31/2023
C	3	10	2/1/2023
A	4	1	2/1/2023
B	5	6	2/1/2023
B	6	9	2/2/2023
A	7	6	2/2/2023
C	8	6	2/3/2023
B	9	10	2/4/2023
A	10	3	2/4/2023
C	11	18	2/6/2023

Table.Pivot

By using the Table.Pivot, values entered in a column of a table can be displayed as separate columns in a wider table. This function is defined in Power Query as follows:

```
Table.Pivot(
        table as table,
        pivotValues as list,
        attributeColumn as text,
        valueColumn as text,
        optional aggregationFunction as nullable function
            ) as table
```

For example, when using this function, instead of writing product names in one column in TableC, different product names can be entered in separate columns and their sales figures can be displayed underneath, as shown in Table 8-91.

Table 8-91. *Example of Table.Pivot*

Date	A	C	B
1/30/2023	17	null	Null
1/31/2023	18	null	Null
2/1/2023	1	10	6
2/2/2023	6	null	9
2/3/2023	null	6	Null
2/4/2023	3	null	10
2/6/2023	null	18	null

This function receives five inputs.

1. In the first input, the reference table is specified.

2. In this input, the names of new columns are entered in a list, such as {"A", "B", "C"}.

3. This input is in text format, and the name of the column that includes the values of new columns (entered in the second input) is entered in the format of text.

4. The column name whose values should be summarized in the new table beneath the new columns is entered in this input as text.

5.   This input is optional and determines how the values are summarized by using functions like `List.Sum` or `List.Average`.

Based on the function explanations and considering TableE, which is equal to TableC after removing the Row column, the result of the following formula is equal to Table 8-92:

```
= Table.Pivot(TableE, {"A", "B", "C"}, "Product Name",
"Quantity", List.Sum)
```

Table 8-92. *Definition of TableE*

Date	A	B	C
1/30/2023	17	null	null
1/31/2023	18	null	null
2/1/2023	1	6	10
2/2/2023	6	9	null
2/3/2023	null	null	6
2/4/2023	3	10	null
2/6/2023	null	null	18

The problem with this formula is that if a product name (such as D) is added to the product list, it will not be automatically added to the result table. Therefore, the second input of this function is modified as follows:

```
= List.Distinct(TableE[Product Name])
```

The output of this function is equal to the list of all product names, so by the following formula, if new products are added to TableE, they are automatically considered:

```
= Table.Pivot(
        TableE,
        List.Distinct(TableE[Product Name]),
        "Product Name",
        "Quantity",
        List.Sum)
```

Table.Unpivot

This function with the following syntax is used to unpivot columns, which means transforming some column headers into a single column and their values into another column in front of them (display the values entered in 2 or more columns under each other in two columns):

```
Table.Unpivot(
        table as table,
        pivotColumns as list,
        attributeColumn as text,
        valueColumn as text
            ) as table
```

Based on the function syntax, it takes four inputs:

1. The first input defines the reference table.

2. In the second input, the titles of the columns for which you want to place their values under two columns are entered as a list.

3. In the third input of this function, the name of first new column (including the title of previous columns) is entered.

4. In the fourth input of this function, the name of the second new column (including the values of previous columns) is entered.

For example, if the values related to the sales of different products is stored in TableF, as shown in Table 8-93, to display them under each other instead of displaying the sales of each product in a separate column, this function can be used as follows:

Table 8-93. *Definition of TableF*

Date	A	C	B
1/30/2023	17	null	null
1/31/2023	18	null	null
2/1/2023	1	10	6
2/2/2023	6	null	9
2/3/2023	null	6	null
2/4/2023	3	null	10
2/6/2023	null	18	null

```
= Table.Unpivot(
        TableF,
        {"A","B","C"},
        "Product Name",
        "Quantity")
```

The result is shown in Table 8-94.

Table 8-94. *Result of Table.Unpivot*

Date	Product Name	Quantity
1/30/2023	A	17
1/31/2023	A	18
2/1/2023	A	1
2/1/2023	C	10
2/1/2023	B	6
2/2/2023	A	6
2/2/2023	B	9
2/3/2023	C	6
2/4/2023	A	3
2/4/2023	B	10
2/6/2023	C	18

By using this formula, columns A, B, and C are collected under a column called Product Name and their sales volumes are displayed in a column called Quantity. Similarly, the Table.UnpivotOtherColumns function can be used to unpivot data, but in the second input of this function, instead of entering a list of column titles that you want to unpivot, you can enter a list of column names that you want to remain unchanged. Therefore, the above function can be revised as follows:

```
= Table.UnpivotOtherColumns(
        TableF,
        {"Date"},
        "Attribute",
        "Value")
```

Table.Group

Table.Group is one of the most important functions in Power Query and it can be used to summarize values in a table. For example, the annual sales per product can be easily extracted from a large database of historical sales by this function. The Table.Group function in Power Query is defined as follows:

```
Table.Group(
        table as table,
        key as any,
        aggregatedColumns as list,
        optional groupKind as nullable number,
        optional comparer as nullable function
            ) as table
```

This function takes five inputs.

1. In the first input, the reference table is entered.

2. The name of the columns you want base the report on are entered in this column. To provide the yearly sales, the name of the column with the values of the years is entered in this input, and to provide the yearly sales by each product, the name of columns with the values of years and product names are entered in a list in this input.

3. In the third input, the name of the columns for applying the calculation and the calculation function are entered in the lists.

4. The fourth input of this function is optional and can define the grouping method as either `GroupKind.Local` (neighbors' values just used for grouping) or `GroupKind.Global` (values across the whole tables are grouped).

5. The fifth input of this function is optional and can be one of the values of `Comparers.Equals`, `Comparer.FromCulture`, `Comparer.Ordinal`, and `Comparer.OrdinalIgnoreCase`.

Based on the function explanation and considering TableC, the result of this function can be seen below.

The following formula results in the sales value by product:

```
= Table.Group(
        TableC,
        "Product Name",
        {"Total",each List.Sum([Quantity])})
```

The result of this formula is in Table 8-95.

Table 8-95. *Result of Table.Group*

Product Name	Total
A	45
C	34
B	25

In the above formula, since no value is entered for the fourth input of this function, the grouping type is considered as `GroupKind.Global`. However, if you enter the grouping type as `GroupKind.Local` in the fourth input of this function, grouping occurs based on the neighbors' product names. The result is shown in Table 8-96.

```
= Table.Group(
        TableC,
        "Product Name",
        {"Total",each List.Sum([Quantity])},
        GroupKind.Local)
```

Table 8-96. *Result of Table.Group*

Product Name	Total
A	35
C	10
A	1
B	15
A	6
C	6
B	10
A	3
C	18

In another example, using the following formula, in addition to calculating the total sales for each product, its average is also calculated:

```
= Table.Group(
        TableC,
        "Product Name",
        {
                {"Total",each List.Sum([Quantity])},
                {"AVG", each List.Average([Quantity])}
        })
```

The result of this formula is as shown in Table 8-97.

Table 8-97. *Result of Table.Group*

Product Name	Total	AVG
A	45	9
C	34	11.33333333
B	25	8.333333333

In this function, to bring the values related to each product in the form of a table next to that product, this function can be used as follows:

```
=Table.Group(
        TableC,
        {"Product Name"},
        {"Count", each _})
```

In this case, the result is shown in Table 8-98.

Table 8-98. *Result of Table.Group*

Product Name	Count
A	[Table]
C	[Table]
B	[Table]

For each product, all rows related to its sales are listed. For example, the table related to product C is visible. See Figure 8-3.

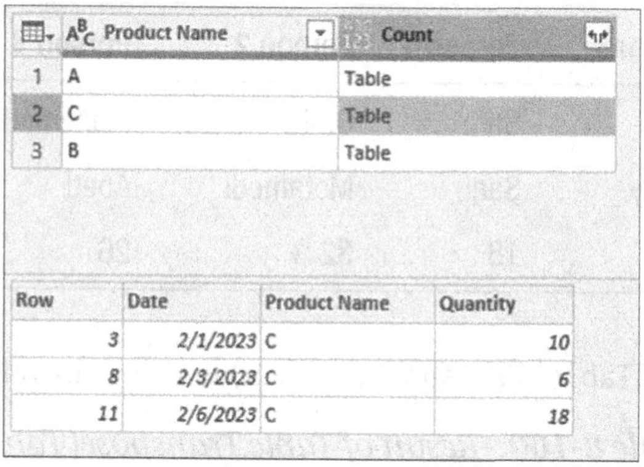

	Product Name	Count
1	A	Table
2	C	Table
3	B	Table

Row	Date	Product Name	Quantity
3	2/1/2023	C	10
8	2/3/2023	C	6
11	2/6/2023	C	18

Figure 8-3. *Product C Information*

Table.Transpose

This function is used to transpose (swap rows and columns of a table) a table as follows:

```
Table.Transpose(
       table as table,
       optional columns as any
              ) as table
```

Based on the function syntax, it takes the two inputs.

1. In the first input, the reference table is entered.
2. The second input of this function is optional and determines the names of columns in the output table.

For example, consider Table 8-99 as TableS.

Table 8-99. *Definition of TableS*

Columns	Person 1	Person 2	Person 3
Name	Sara	Omid	Mohamad
Family	Sani	Motamedi	Abed
Age	18	32	26

The result of Table.Transpose(TableS) is shown in Table 8-100.

Table 8-100. *Result of Table.Transpose(TableS)*

Column1	Column2	Column3
Name	Family	Age
Sara	Sani	18
Omid	Motamedi	32
Mohamad	Abed	26

And the result of

```
= Table.Transpose(TableS,{"Name","Family","Age"})
```

is shown in Table 8-101.

Table 8-101. *Result of Table.Transpose*

Name	Family	Age
Name	Family	Age
Sara	Sani	18
Omid	Motamedi	32
Mohamad	Abed	26

Combining Tables

There are two methods for combining tables. In the first method, which is known as appending, the values of two tables are placed under each other. For example, table one is the sales values for 2019 and table two is the sales values for 2020. By appending these two tables, a new table is created including the sales values in both the years 2019 and 2020.

However, sometimes it is necessary to bring the values from a column of Table A and display it in a new column in Table B. For example, if the values of product prices are in Table A and Table B include the historical sales volume, to calculate the total sales in dollar, it is necessary to call the price from Table A and display it in Table B. This method of combining tables, which ends with adding new columns to the reference table, is called merging.

In this section, the functions related to both methods of combining tables are discussed.

Table.Combine

Table.Combine is used to append two or more tables in Power Query as follows:

```
Table.Combine(
        tables as list,
        optional columns as any
            ) as table
```

This function receives two inputs.

1. In the first input, the tables that you want to append are mentioned as the separate values of a list.

2. In the second input of this function, the list of column names that you want to display in the output table is defined. This input is optional; if no value is entered, all columns of the tables (common and non-common) are displayed in the output.

For this example, consider TableH, TableI, and TableJ (shown in Tables 8-102, 8-103, and 8-104, respectively).

Table 8-102. *Definition of TableH*

Row	Date	Product Name	Quantity
1	1/30/2023	A	17
2	1/31/2023	A	18
3	2/1/2023	C	10
4	2/1/2023	A	1

Table 8-103. *Definition of TableI*

Row	Date	Product Name	Quantity
5	2/1/2023	B	6
6	2/2/2023	B	9
7	2/2/2023	A	6
8	2/3/2023	C	6

Table 8-104. *Definition of Table J*

Row	Date	Product Name	Quantity
9	2/4/2023	B	10
10	2/4/2023	A	3
11	2/6/2023	C	18

In this case, the result of = `Table.Combine({TableH,TableI,TableJ})` is shown in Table 8-105.

Table 8-105. *Result of Table.Combine*

Row	Date	Product Name	Quantity
1	1/30/2023	A	17
2	1/31/2023	A	18
3	2/1/2023	C	10
4	2/1/2023	A	1
5	2/1/2023	B	6
6	2/2/2023	B	9
7	2/2/2023	A	6
8	2/3/2023	C	6
9	2/4/2023	B	10
10	2/4/2023	A	3
11	2/6/2023	C	18

The result of = `Table.Combine({TableH,TableI,TableJ},{"Date", "Quantity"})` is presented in Table 8-106.

Table 8-106. *Result of Table.Combine*

Date	Quantity
1/30/2023	17
1/31/2023	18
2/1/2023	10
2/1/2023	1
2/1/2023	6
2/2/2023	9
2/2/2023	6
2/3/2023	6
2/4/2023	10
2/4/2023	3
2/6/2023	18

In a similar example, if the name of column Product Name in table J is changed to Products, the result of the formula = `Table.Combine({TableH, TableI,TableJ})` would be equal to Table 8-107.

Table 8-107. *Result of Table.Combine*

Row	Date	Product Name	Quantity	ProductS
1	1/30/2023	A	17	null
2	1/31/2023	A	18	null
3	2/1/2023	C	10	null
4	2/1/2023	A	1	null
5	2/1/2023	B	6	null
6	2/2/2023	B	9	null
7	2/2/2023	A	6	null
8	2/3/2023	C	6	null
9	2/4/2023	Null	10	B
10	2/4/2023	Null	3	A
11	2/6/2023	Null	18	C

Another way of combine tables, instead of using Table.Combine, is to use the & operator, as follows:

```
= TableH & TableI & TableJ
```

The result of this formula is the same as the following formula:

```
= Table.Combine ({TableH, TableI, TableJ})
```

Table.Join

To merge tables (add columns of one table to another table as new columns), Table.Join can be used. To match the rows of the tables, both tables should include a common column (such as product ID or customer ID) with the same format and common values. This function can be used as follows:

```
Table.Join(
        table1 as table,
        key1 as any,
        table2 as table,
        key2 as any,
        optional joinKind as nullable number,
        optional joinAlgorithm as nullable number,
        optional keyEqualityComparers as nullable list
            ) as table
```

Based on the function syntax, it takes the following inputs:

1. The first input specifies the reference table (Table A) to which new columns will be added.

2. In the second input, the name of the common column in the reference table is entered as a text value.

3. The name of the second table (Table B), from which the values should be extracted, is entered in the third input.

4. In the fourth input, the name of the common column in the second table is entered.

5. The fifth input, known as joinKind, determines the merging model by entering one of these values:

    JoinKind.Inner

    JoinKind.LeftOuter

    JoinKind.RightOuter

    JoinKind.FullOuter

    JoinKind.LeftAnti

    JoinKind.RightAnti

6. The sixth input is optional and determines the algorithm for calculation and can be one of the values in Table 8-108.

Table 8-108. *Types of Join Algorithms*

Algorithm	Value
JoinAlgorithm.Dynamic	0
JoinAlgorithm.PairwiseHash	1
JoinAlgorithm.SortMerge	2
JoinAlgorithm.LeftHash	3
JoinAlgorithm.RightHash	4
JoinAlgorithm.LeftIndex	5
JoinAlgorithm.RightIndex	6

7. The seventh input of this function is also optional
    and determines the comparison criterion by
    entering one of the following values:

    Comparer.Equals

    Comparer.FromCulture

    Comparer.Ordinal

    Comparer.OrdinalIgnoreCase

For example, consider TableP as shown in Table 8-109.

Table 8-109. *Definition of TableP*

Date	Product	Quantity
3/21/2021	A	5
3/21/2021	B	4
3/23/2021	A	3
3/23/2021	C	5
3/24/2021	D	1

TabelQ is shown in Table 8-110.

Table 8-110. *Definition of TableQ*

Product Name	Price
A	100
B	150
E	200
F	100

If products A and B are both present on the two tables, and product A has been repeated twice in the first table, the result of the following formula is shown in Table 8-111:

```
= Table.Join(TableP,"Product",TableQ,"Prod
uct Name")
```

Table 8-111.   Result of Table.Join

Date	Product	Quantity	Product Name	Price
3/21/2021	A	5	A	100
3/23/2021	A	3	A	100
3/21/2021	B	4	B	150

In the above formula, the type of merger is not specified, and in this case, the default method of merging, which is known as inner merger, is applied, which will lead to a table for the rows with the product name that existed in both tables.

To explain inner merge, consider Figure 8-4. The left circle represents the names of the products listed in the first table and the right circle represents the names of the products listed in the second table. In this example, two products, A and B, are listed in both tables (shown in the common area of two circles).

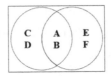

Figure 8-4. *Table members*

Therefore, the result of the above formula is equal to the intersection area between two tables, which is highlighted in Figure 8-5.

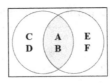

Figure 8-5. *Intersection area*

By changing the merging method (fifth input), different results will be achieved, as you can see in Table 8-112.

Table 8-112. *Different Types of Joins*

JoinKind.Inner

JoinKind.LeftOuter

JoinKind.RightOuter

JoinKind.FullOuter

JoinKind.LeftAnti

JoinKind.RightAnti

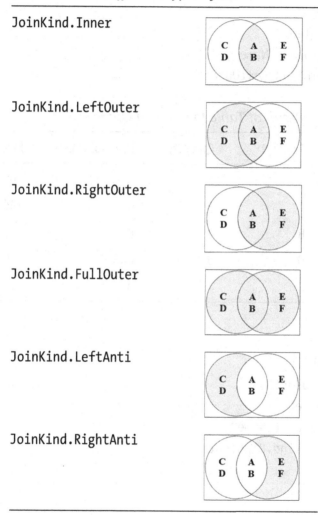

The results of this function in different scenarios are presented in the following examples (see Tables 8-113 through 8-117).

```
= Table.Join(TableP,
        "Product",
        TableQ,
        "Product Name",
        JoinKind.LeftOuter)
```

Table 8-113. *Result of Table.Join in Left Outer*

Date	Product	Quantity	Product Name	Price
3/21/2021	A	5	A	100
3/23/2021	A	3	A	100
3/21/2021	B	4	B	150
3/23/2021	C	5	null	null
3/24/2021	D	1	null	null

```
= Table.Join(
        TableP,
        "Product",
        TableQ,
        "Product Name",
        JoinKind.RightOuter)
```

Table 8-114. *Result of Table.Join in Right Outer*

Date	Product	Quantity	Product Name	Price
3/21/2021	A	5	A	100
3/23/2021	A	3	A	100
3/21/2021	B	4	B	150
Null	null	null	E	200
Null	null	null	F	100

```
= Table.Join(
        TableP,
        "Product",
        TableQ,
        "Product Name",
        JoinKind.FullOuter)
```

Table 8-115. *Result of Table.Join in Full Outer*

Date	Product	Quantity	Product Name	Price
3/21/2021	A	5	A	100
3/23/2021	A	3	A	100
3/21/2021	B	4	B	150
3/23/2021	C	5	null	null
3/24/2021	D	1	null	null
Null	null	null	E	200
Null	null	null	F	100

```
= Table.Join(
        TableP,
        "Product",
        TableQ,
        "Product Name",
        JoinKind.LeftAnti)
```

Table 8-116. *Result of Table.Join in Left Anti*

Date	Product	Quantity	Product Name	Price
3/23/2021	C	5	null	null
3/24/2021	D	1	null	null

```
= Table.Join(
        TableP,
        "Product",
        TableQ,
        "Product Name",
        JoinKind.RightAnti)
```

Table 8-117. *Result of Table.Join in Right Anti*

Date	Product	Quantity	Product Name	Price
null	null	null	E	200
null	null	null	F	100

The main drawback of this function is that the column names in the first and second tables must be completely unique and distinct. If there is a column with the same name in both tables, this function will result in an error.

Table.NestedJoin

Table.NestedJoin is like the Table.Join function; the difference is that in the output of this function, the related rows in the second table are added to a column in the first table as values in the format of the table. Since the name of the new column is specified by the user, if the tables have columns with the same name, the output of this function is not an error.

This function is defined in the query as follows:

```
Table.NestedJoin(
table1 as table,
key1 as any,
table2 as any,
key2 as any,
newColumnName as text,
optional joinKind as nullable number,
optional keyEqualityComparers as nullable list
) as table
```

Based on the function syntax, it takes the following inputs:

1. The first input specifies the reference table (Table A) where you want the new column added.

2. In the second input, the name of the common column in the reference table is entered as a text value.

3. The name of the second table (Table B), from which the values should be extracted, is entered in this input.

4. In this input, the name of the common column in the second table is entered.

5. The name of the new column is determined as a text in this input.

6. This input, known as `joinKind`, determines the merging model entering one of the following values:

`JoinKind.Inner`

`JoinKind.LeftOuter`

`JoinKind.RightOuter`

`JoinKind.FullOuter`

`JoinKind.LeftAnti`

`JoinKind.RightAnti`

7. The seventh input of this function is optional and determines the comparison criterion entering one of the following values:

`Comparer.Equals`

`Comparer.FromCulture`

`Comparer.Ordinal`

`Comparer.OrdinalIgnoreCase`

Given the function explanation, the result of the following formula is equal to the first table in which a new column named New Data has been added (see Table 8-118):

```
= Table.NestedJoin(
        TableP,
        "Product",
        TableQ,
        "Product Name",
        "New Data")
```

Table 8-118. *Result of Table.NestedJoin*

Date	Product	Quantity	New Data
3/21/2021	A	5	[Table]
3/21/2021	B	4	[Table]
3/23/2021	A	3	[Table]
3/23/2021	C	5	[Table]
3/24/2021	D	1	[Table]

As seen, the New Data column only contains the table expression. By clicking the first value of this column, the data summary will be displayed, as shown in Figure 8-6.

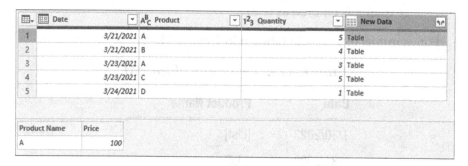

Figure 8-6. *Displaying table data values*

Expanding Columns

In the case that values in a column are in the format of list, record, or table, the functions of this section can be used to expand such values.

Table.ExpandListColumn

If one of the columns in the table contains information of type list, this function can be used as follows to expand the values as new rows:

```
Table.ExpandListColumn(
        table as table,
        column as text
             ) as table
```

This function is very simple and receives two inputs.

1. The first input specifies the reference table.

2. In the second input, the column name, including the values in the format of list that you want to expand, is entered as text.

For example, use TableM (shown in Table 8-119).

Table 8-119. *Definition of TableM*

Date	Product Name
1/30/2023	[List]
1/31/2023	[List]
2/1/2023	[List]
2/2/2023	[List]
2/3/2023	[List]
2/4/2023	[List]
2/6/2023	[List]

In the Product Name column, the names of the products sold on that date are listed. For example, in Figure 8-7, the list of products sold on the date 2/1/2023 is displayed.

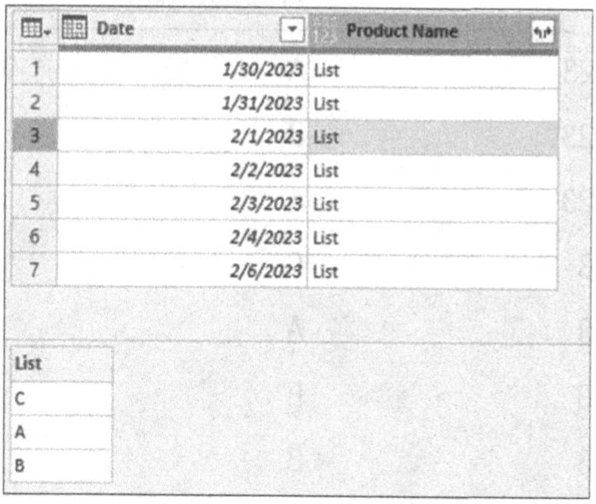

	Date		Product Name	
1	1/30/2023	List		
2	1/31/2023	List		
3	2/1/2023	List		
4	2/2/2023	List		
5	2/3/2023	List		
6	2/4/2023	List		
7	2/6/2023	List		

List
C
A
B

Figure 8-7. *Displaying data members in list format*

To display these values as new rows, the following formula can be used:

```
= Table.ExpandListColumn(TableM,"Product Name")
```

The results are shown in Table 8-120.

Table 8-120. *Result of Table.ExpandListColumn*

Date	Product Name
1/30/2023	A
1/30/2023	B
1/31/2023	A
2/1/2023	C
2/1/2023	A
2/1/2023	B
2/2/2023	B
2/2/2023	A
2/3/2023	C
2/4/2023	B
2/4/2023	A
2/6/2023	C

Table.ExpandRecordColumn

To expand the values entered in the format of records in a table, Table.
ExpandRecordColumn can be used as follows:

```
Table.ExpandRecordColumn(
        table as table,
        column as text,
        fieldNames as list,
        optional newColumnNames as nullable list
                ) as table
```

This function receives four inputs.

1. The first input is the reference table.

2. In the second input, the name of the column containing record values is entered as text.

3. In the third input, the names of the fields you want to extract from the records are entered as a list.

4. This input is optional and is used to define the new names for the extracted columns.

For example, he values in the TableN are as shown in Table 8-121.

Table 8-121. *Definition of TableN*

Date	Info
1/30/2023	[Record]
1/31/2023	[Record]
2/1/2023	[Record]
2/2/2023	[Record]
2/3/2023	[Record]
2/4/2023	[Record]
2/6/2023	[Record]

Here the values related to sales (including product name and quantity) for each date are entered as records in the Info column. Figure 8-8 shows the details of the record entered in the Info column for the date of 2023/2/2.

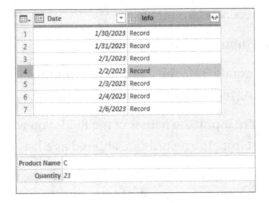

Figure 8-8. *Display of record data*

To extract the values of this column, the following formula can be used:

```
= Table.ExpandRecordColumn(TableN,"Info",{"Quantity"})
```

The result of this formula is as shown in Table 8-122.

Table 8-122. *Result of Table.ExpandRecordColumn*

Date	Quantity
1/30/2023	10
1/31/2023	3
2/1/2023	5
2/2/2023	21
2/3/2023	11
2/4/2023	12
2/6/2023	8

Similarly, the result of

```
= Table.ExpandRecordColumn(TableN,
        "Info",
        {"Product Name","Quantity"})
```

is shown in Table 8-123.

Table 8-123. *Result of Table.ExpandRecordColumn*

Date	Product Name	Quantity
1/30/2023	A	10
1/31/2023	B	3
2/1/2023	A	5
2/2/2023	C	21
2/3/2023	C	11
2/4/2023	A	12
2/6/2023	B	8

Similarly, to change the names of new columns, the following formula can be used:

```
= Table.ExpandRecordColumn(
        TableN,
        "Info",
        {"Product Name","Quantity"},
        {"X1","X2"})
```

In this case, the result is shown in Table 8-124.

Table 8-124. *Result of Table.ExpandRecordColumn*

Date	X1	X2
1/30/2023	A	10
1/31/2023	B	3
2/1/2023	A	5
2/2/2023	C	21
2/3/2023	C	11
2/4/2023	A	12
2/6/2023	B	8

Table.ExpandTableColumn

To expand the values in the format of a table, entered in a column, this function can be used as follows:

```
Table.ExpandTableColumn(
            table as table,
            column as text,
            columnNames as list,
            optional newColumnNames as nullable list
            ) as table
```

This function receives four inputs.

1. The reference table is entered in the first input.

2. The name of the column you want to expand the values of (in the format of table) is entered in this input.

3. In this input, it is determined which columns of the tables determined in the second input should be extracted.

4. This input is optional and is used to change the name of extracted columns.

For example, consider TableO (shown in Table 8-125).

Table 8-125. *Definition of TableO*

Date	Info
1/30/2023	[Table]
1/31/2023	[Table]
2/1/2023	[Table]

The product names and sales quantity for each date are presented in the format of the table in front of each table. Figure 8-9 shows the entered values for the last date.

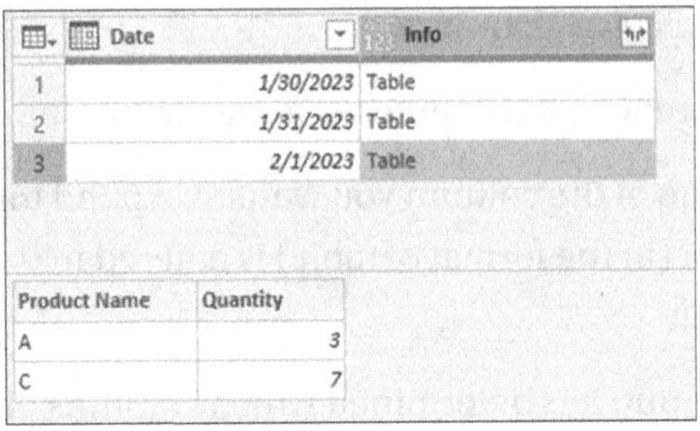

Figure 8-9. *Display of table data*

To extract the values from the Info column, this function can be used as follows:

```
= Table.ExpandTableColumn(
        Table0,
        "Info",
        {"Product Name","Quantity"})
```

The result is shown in Table 8-126.

Table 8-126. *Result of Table.ExpandTableColumn in Left Outer*

Date	Product Name	Quantity
1/30/2023	A	2
1/30/2023	B	12
1/30/2023	C	6
1/31/2023	B	8
1/31/2023	C	9
2/1/2023	A	3
2/1/2023	C	7

Table.AggregateTableColumn

Instead of extracting values from the tables entered in the Info column, the summary of values can be extracted by using `Table.AggregateTableColumn`. This function can be used as follows:

```
Table.AggregateTableColumn(
        table as table,
        column as text,
        aggregations as list
           ) as table
```

Based on the function syntax, it takes three inputs.

1. In the first input, the reference table is specified.

2. The name of the column that includes the values in the format of the table is entered in this input.

3. In this input, you list three values: the name of column you want to summarize, the operation for summarizing the values, and the name of new column in the result table. So `{{"A",List.Sum,"X"}}` means that by using the `List.Sum` function, values from column A are used and their summation result in a new column, namely X.

To examine the performance of this function, use Table0. In this case, the results of this function in different formulas are shown in Tables 8-127 and 8-128.

```
= Table.AggregateTableColumn(
        Table0,
        "Info",
        {{"Quantity",List.Sum,"Sum of Quantity"}})
```

Table 8-127. *Result of Table.AggregateTableColumn*

Date	Sum of Quantity
1/30/2023	20
1/31/2023	17
2/1/2023	10

= Table.AggregateTableColumn(

```
Table0,
"Info",
{{"Quantity",List.Sum,"Sum of Quantity"},
        {"Quantity",List.Average,"Average of
        Quantity"},
        {"Product",List.Count,"Count of Product"}})
```

Table 8-128. *Result of Table.AggregateTableColumn*

Date	Sum of Quantity	Average of Quantity	Count of Product
1/30/2023	20	6.666666667	3
1/31/2023	17	8.5	2
2/1/2023	10	5	2

Replacing Column Values

In this section, functions related to replacing values in table columns with new values are presented.

Table.FillDown and Table.FillUp

Functions Table.FillDown and Table.FillUp are used to fill null cells with the value of the above or below cells, as follows:

```
Table.FillDown(
        table as table,
        columns as list
            ) as table
Table.FillUp(
        table as table,
        columns as list
            ) as table
```

These two functions receive two inputs.

1. In the first input, the reference table is specified.

2. The name of the column or columns that you want to apply the function to is entered in this input as a list format.

Based on the function explanation and considering TableL (shown in Table 8-129),

Table 8-129. *Definition of TableL*

Row	Date	Product Name	Quantity
1	1/30/2023	A	17
2	null	A	18
3	2/1/2023	C	10
4	null	A	1
5	null	B	6
6	2/2/2023	B	9
7	null	A	6
8	2/3/2023	C	6
9	2/4/2023	B	10
10	null	A	3
11	2/6/2023	C	18

the result of = `Table.FillDown(TableL,{"Date"})` is shown in Table 8-130.

Table 8-130. *Result of Table.FillDown*

Row	Date	Product Name	Quantity
1	1/30/2023	A	17
2	1/30/2023	A	18
3	2/1/2023	C	10
4	2/1/2023	A	1
5	2/1/2023	B	6

(continued)

Table 8-130. (*continued*)

Row	Date	Product Name	Quantity
6	2/2/2023	B	9
7	2/2/2023	A	6
8	2/3/2023	C	6
9	2/4/2023	B	10
10	2/4/2023	A	3
11	2/6/2023	C	18

The result of the following formula is shown in Table 8-131:

```
= Table.FillUp(TableL,{"Date"})
```

Table 8-131. *Result of Table.FillUp*

Row	Date	Product Name	Quantity
1	1/30/2023	A	17
2	2/1/2023	A	18
3	2/1/2023	C	10
4	2/2/2023	A	1
5	2/2/2023	B	6
6	2/2/2023	B	9
7	2/3/2023	A	6
8	2/3/2023	C	6
9	2/4/2023	B	10
10	2/6/2023	A	3
11	2/6/2023	C	18

Table.ReplaceErrorValues

This function is used to replace error values in one or more columns of a table with new values as follows:

```
Table.ReplaceErrorValues(
    table as table,
    errorReplacement as list
        ) as table
```

This function receives two inputs.

1. The first input is the reference table.

2. In the second input, the name of columns and values that should replace the error values in each column are entered in lists with two values. For example, to replace error values in column A with the value NEW Value1, this input is entered as {"A","New Value1"}, and to replace error values in column B with New Value2 simultaneously, this input can be defined as follows:
   ={{"A","New Value1"},{"B","New Value2"}}

To check the application of this function, consider Table 8-132 as TableR.

Table 8-132. *Definitoin of TableR*

Row	Date	Product Name	Quantity	Rank
2	1/31/2023	A	18	1
11	2/6/2023	Error	18	1
1	1/30/2023	A	17	2
3	2/1/2023	C	10	3
9	2/4/2023	B	10	3
6	2/2/2023	Error	9	4
5	2/1/2023	B	Error	5
7	2/2/2023	A	6	5
8	2/3/2023	C	6	5
10	2/4/2023	A	Error	6
4	2/1/2023	A	1	Error

So, the following formulas come with different results. See Tables 8-133 and 8-134.

```
Table.ReplaceErrorValues(
        TableR,
        {"Product Name","New Value1"})
```

Table 8-133. *Result of Table.ReplaceErrorValues*

Row	Date	Product Name	Quantity	Rank
2	1/31/2023	A	18	1
11	2/6/2023	New Value1	18	1
1	1/30/2023	A	17	2
3	2/1/2023	C	10	3
9	2/4/2023	B	10	3
6	2/2/2023	New Value1	9	4
5	2/1/2023	B	Error	5
7	2/2/2023	A	6	5
8	2/3/2023	C	6	5
10	2/4/2023	A	Error	6
4	2/1/2023	A	1	Error

```
Table.ReplaceErrorValues(
TableR,
{
        {"Product Name","New Value1"},
        {"Quantity","New Value2"},
        {"rank","New Value3"}
})
```

Table 8-134. *Result of Table.ReplaceErrorValues*

Row	Date	Product Name	Quantity	rank
2	1/31/2023	A	18	1
11	2/6/2023	New Value1	18	1
1	1/30/2023	A	17	2
3	2/1/2023	C	10	3
9	2/4/2023	B	10	3
6	2/2/2023	New Value1	9	4
5	2/1/2023	B	New Value2	5
7	2/2/2023	A	6	5
8	2/3/2023	C	6	5
10	2/4/2023	A	New Value2	6
4	2/1/2023	A	1	New Value3

Table.ReplaceValue

To replace the values recorded in the columns of a table with new values, the Table.ReplaceValue can be used as follows.

```
Table.ReplaceValue(
        table as table,
        oldValue as any,
        newValue as any,
        replacer as function,
        columnsToSearch as list
            ) as table
```

This function receives five inputs:

1. In the first input of this function, the reference table is defined.

2. In the second input, the value that you want to replace with a new one is entered.

3. In the third input of this function, the new value is entered.

4. The type of replacement function is determined in this input. To replace one text with another, `Replacer.ReplaceText` is entered, and to replace a number with a number, `Replacer.ReplaceValue` is entered.

5. In this input, the names of columns on which the replacements should be applied are entered as a list.

Based on the function explanations, to replace the name of product A with Mobile in TableC, the following formula can be used. See Table 8-135.

```
= Table.ReplaceValue(
        TableC,
        "A",
        "Mobile",
        Replacer.ReplaceText,
        {"Product Name"})
```

Table 8-135. *Result of Table.ReplaceValue*

Row	Date	Product Name	Quantity
1	1/30/2023	Mobile	17
2	1/31/2023	Mobile	18
3	2/1/2023	C	10
4	2/1/2023	Mobile	1
5	2/1/2023	B	6
6	2/2/2023	B	9
7	2/2/2023	Mobile	6
8	2/3/2023	C	6
9	2/4/2023	B	10
10	2/4/2023	Mobile	3
11	2/6/2023	C	18

Or in a similar situation, to replace the number 1 with the number 100 in the Quantity and Row columns, the following formula can be used. See Table 8-136.

```
= Table.ReplaceValue(
        TableC,
        1,
        100,
        Replacer.ReplaceValue,
        {"Row","Quantity"})
```

Table 8-136. *Result of Table.ReplaceValue*

Row	Date	Product Name	Quantity
100	1/30/2023	A	17
2	1/31/2023	A	18
3	2/1/2023	C	10
4	2/1/2023	A	100
5	2/1/2023	B	6
6	2/2/2023	B	9
7	2/2/2023	A	6
8	2/3/2023	C	6
9	2/4/2023	B	10
10	2/4/2023	A	3
11	2/6/2023	C	18

Finding a Value in a Table

In this section, the functions related to determining the location of values in the table are presented.

Table.FindText

This function is used to extract rows from a table that contain a specific text. This function is defined in Power Query as follows:

```
Table.FindText(
    table as table,
    text as text
    ) as table
```

`Table.FindText` receives two inputs.

1. The first input of this function is the reference table.

2. The text that you are searching for is entered in the second input.

The output of the function is the rows of the reference table that include the searching text. Therefore, the result of the formula = `Table.FindText(TableC, "A")` is equal to Table 8-137.

Table 8-137. *Result of Table.FindText*

Row	Date	Product Name	Quantity
1	1/30/2023	A	17
2	1/31/2023	A	18
4	2/1/2023	A	1
7	2/2/2023	A	6
10	2/4/2023	A	3

Table.PositionOf

`Table.PositionOf` is used to extract the number of rows including specific values, as follows:

```
Table.PositionOf(
        table as table,
        row as record,
        optional occurrence as any,
        optional equationCriteria as any
            ) as any
```

This function receives four inputs as follows:

1. The reference table is entered in the first input of this function.

2. The second input is defined as a record and specifies the rows you are searching for. For example, [a=1] is entered if you are searching for the number of rows with the value of 1 in the column named a.

3. This input is optional and specifies which occurrence should be displayed as output via Occurrence.First, Occurrence.Last, Occurrence.All, Occurrence.Optional, Occurrence.Required, or Occurrence.Repeating.

4. This input is optional and allows you to specify custom criteria for comparing the values.

The result of this function is always a number indicating the row number with the desired conditions. If the desired row is not found, the output of this function is -1.

Consider TableT (shown in Table 8-138).

Table 8-138. *Definition of TableT*

Product Name	Quantity
A	1
B	3
A	2
B	3
A	2
C	1
A	2
C	3
B	2

The result of this function in the following formula is equal to the number 6, meaning that the row with the product name equal to C and a quantity of 1 is in the seventh row of the table:

```
= Table.PositionOf(TableT,[Product Name="C",Quantity=1])
```

Similarly, the result of the following formula is equal to 2. It is true that the product name A is registered in the third row and its Quantity column is 2, but since it is not specified which occurrence is desired in the third input, the first occurrence is displayed in the output.

```
= Table.PositionOf(
TableT,
[Product Name="A",Quantity=2])
```

If you want to display all occurrences in the output, use the following formula:

```
= Table.PositionOf(
TableT,
[Product Name="A",Quantity=2]
,Occurrence.All)
```

Table.PositionOfAny

Table.PositionOfAny is like the Table.PositionOfAny function, with the difference that in the second input of this function, several conditions can be defined like

> {[Product Name="A",Quantity=2], [Product
> Name="C",Quantity=1]}

This function is defined in Power Query as follows:

```
Table.PositionOfAny(
       table as table,
       rows as list,
       optional occurrence as nullable number,
       optional equationCriteria as any
             ) as any
```

According to the function explanations, the result of the following formula is equal to a list in the form of {2,4,5,6}:

```
= Table.PositionOfAny(
       TableT,
       {
```

```
        [Product Name="A",Quantity=2],
        [Product Name="C",Quantity=1]
    },
    Occurrence.All)
```

Summary

This chapter was a journey through the intricate landscape of table functions within Power Query, providing a comprehensive understanding of how tables serve as the foundation for structured data analysis and manipulation.

The chapter commenced with a fundamental exploration of tables as dynamic data containers. You grasped the essence of columns and rows, understanding how Power Query views tables as versatile structures capable of holding diverse data types and relationships. Through this, you learned to manually create tables and generate them through calculated expressions.

As you delved deeper, you uncovered the transformative power of table functions. These functions empower you to filter, sort, reshape, and aggregate data within tables with precision. The art of crafting tables that align with your analytical goals became second nature, enhancing your data manipulation abilities.

The chapter led you into the realm of table relationships, where data connections unveiled themselves. You explored techniques for joining, merging, and relating tables, piecing together data from diverse sources to weave coherent narratives. This skillset allows you to unearth insights that span multiple datasets.

Furthermore, you delved into the world of data enrichment and summarization. The potential of these functions came to light as you discovered how to distill complex datasets into concise, insightful summaries. This skill empowers you to identify trends, patterns, and anomalies hidden within the data.

Throughout the chapter, practical examples were seamlessly integrated to illustrate the real-world application of table functions. As you concluded this chapter, you emerged with the ability to transform raw data into organized narratives of knowledge. Your newfound mastery of table manipulation can redefine your approach to data analysis, offering a deeper understanding of relationships, trends, and opportunities.

In the next chapter, the functions for extracting the values and tables from different data sources are presented. You will learn how to connect Power Query with different data sources and extract the desired info from the data sources.

CHAPTER 9

Extracting from Data Sources

In the dynamic landscape of data-driven decision-making, information resides in diverse corners of the digital world. Whether it's buried in spreadsheets, residing in databases, or streaming from APIs, the ability to extract, unify, and analyze data from these sources is paramount. Welcome to a chapter dedicated to the mastery of Power Query's data source functions, which are your passport to seamlessly accessing and harnessing information from various origins, transforming it into the fuel that powers informed choices.

Data, in its multitude of forms, fuels the engine of modern business and research. But data is often dispersed across a spectrum of platforms, each with its own structure, language, and rules. Power Query's data source functions emerge as the bridge that connects these disparate islands of information, paving the way for unified analysis.

Your journey through this chapter begins with a fundamental exploration of data source functions: the tools that enable Power Query to communicate with different data origins. You'll delve into the world of connectors, each designed to interpret the language of a specific data source.

© Omid Motamedisedeh 2024
O. Motamedisedeh, *The Ultimate Guide to Functions in Power Query*,
https://doi.org/10.1007/978-1-4842-9754-4_9

Folder.Contents

Using Folder.Contents, values stored in files with various formats (such as .xlsx, .accdb, .txt, and CSV) in a folder can be called as follows:

```
Folder.Contents(
      path as text,
      optional options as nullable record
      ) as table
```

According to the above explanation, this function takes these two inputs:

1. In the first input of this function, the path of folder is entered.

2. The second input of this function is optional and is set as a record for settings.

Based on the above explanation, if various files are stored in a specific path such as C:\Users\omid_\OneDrive\Desktop\Data, as in Figure 9-1,

Name		Status	Date modified
05-Inventory		⊗	2/23/2023 7:09 PM
05-Inventory		⊗	2/23/2023 7:10 PM
05-Inventory		⊗	2/23/2023 7:09 PM
06-Inventory		⊗	8/29/2018 6:27 PM
06-Inventory		⊗	8/29/2018 6:12 PM
06-Inventory		⊗	2/23/2023 7:09 PM
07-Article		⊗	8/7/2020 9:06 PM

Figure 9-1. Folder contents

the result of the following formula will be equal to Figure 9-2:

```
= Folder.Contents("C:\Users\omid_\OneDrive\
Desktop\Data")
```

	Content	Aᵇ꜀ Name	Aᵇ꜀ Extension	Date accessed	Date modified	Date created	Attributes
1	Binary	05-Inventory.csv	csv	2/23/2023 7:10:17 PM	2/23/2023 7:09:46 PM	2/23/2023 7:09:46 PM	Record
2	Binary	05-Inventory.txt	txt	2/23/2023 7:10:23 PM	2/23/2023 7:10:05 PM	2/23/2023 7:07:14 PM	Record
3	Binary	05-Inventory.xlsx	xlsx	2/23/2023 7:09:24 PM	2/23/2023 7:09:23 PM	2/23/2023 7:09:23 PM	Record
4	Binary	06-Inventory.csv	csv	2/23/2023 7:07:51 PM	8/29/2018 6:27:30 PM	2/23/2023 7:07:14 PM	Record
5	Binary	06-Inventory.txt	txt	2/23/2023 7:10:18 PM	8/29/2018 6:12:03 PM	2/23/2023 7:07:14 PM	Record
6	Binary	06-Inventory.xlsx	xlsx	2/23/2023 7:09:24 PM	2/23/2023 7:09:22 PM	2/23/2023 7:08:08 PM	Record
7	Binary	07-Article.pdf	pdf	2/23/2023 7:07:48 PM	8/7/2020 5:05:32 PM	2/23/2023 7:07:14 PM	Record

Figure 9-2. *Data called from a specific address*

In the output of this function, the Content column is the most important one. It includes the values stored in the relevant files at the entered address. By using the functions explain in the rest of this chapter, these values can be extracted.

Csv.Document

By using `Folder.Contents` to load values from text or CSV files, saved in a specific path, the information will be shown in the format of binary in the column with the name "content". To extract such values, `CSV.Document` can be used as follows:

```
Csv.Document(
source as any,
optional columns as any,
optional delimiter as any,
optional extraValues as nullable number,
optional encoding as nullable number
) as table
```

This function takes these five inputs:

1. In the first input, a binary value, including the values of a CSV or text file, is entered.

2. The second input is optional, and the column names can be entered into it.

3. The third input of this function is optional, and the values separator can be specified by it.

4. This input specifies the text encoding used in the CSV file.

5. The last input allows the user to specify how Power Query should handle rows in the CSV file that contain more or fewer values than the defined columns, by entering 0,1 or 2.

According to the function explanations, and considering the previous example after removing all the columns except Content, Name, and Extension and then calling its result as #"Removed Other Columns", then using CSV.Document as

> = Table.AddColumn(#"Removed Other Columns",
>
> "Custom",
>
> each CSV.Document([Content]))

results in the information shown in Figure 9-3.

	Content	A^B_C Name	A^B_C Extension	Custom
1	Binary	05-Inventory.csv	.csv	Table
2	Binary	05-Inventory.txt	.txt	Table
3	Binary	05-Inventory.xlsx	.xlsx	Table
4	Binary	06-Inventory.csv	.csv	Table
5	Binary	06-Inventory.txt	.txt	Table
6	Binary	06-Inventory.xlsx	.xlsx	Table
7	Binary	07-Article.pdf	.pdf	Table

Figure 9-3. *CSV.Document function result*

As you can see, the word Table is shown in the new column in all rows. By selecting the value of this column in front of the CSV or text files (rows 1, 2, 4, and 5), the values inside that file will be displayed correctly, as shown in Figure 9-4.

	Content	A^B_C Name	A^B_C Extension	Custom
1	Binary	05-Inventory.csv	.csv	Table
2	Binary	05-Inventory.txt	.txt	Table
3	Binary	05-Inventory.xlsx	.xlsx	Table
4	Binary	06-Inventory.csv	.csv	Table
5	Binary	06-Inventory.txt	.txt	Table
6	Binary	06-Inventory.xlsx	.xlsx	Table
7	Binary	07-Article.pdf	.pdf	Table

Column1	Column2	Column3
last update on 2018/02/19		
Product ID	Color ID	inventory
846-3	YE-4	5971
995-9	YE-4	4655
971-6	RE-4	2121
805-2	GE-4	4808
802-8	YE-3	6448
853-3	BU-2	7276

Figure 9-4. *Result of the function for CSV tables*

But, by selecting the value of this column in the row where the data format is XLSX (Excel file), the result will be disordered and displayed as shown in Figure 9-5.

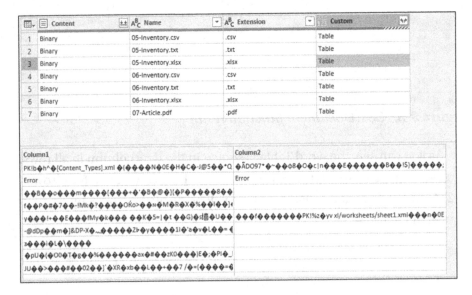

Figure 9-5. Result of the function for Excel tables

The same result can be shown by selecting the Table in the rows for PDF files. See Figure 9-6.

	Content	AB꜀ Name	AB꜀ Extension	Custom
1	Binary	05-Inventory.csv	.csv	Table
2	Binary	05-Inventory.txt	.txt	Table
3	Binary	05-Inventory.xlsx	.xlsx	Table
4	Binary	06-Inventory.csv	.csv	Table
5	Binary	06-Inventory.txt	.txt	Table
6	Binary	06-Inventory.xlsx	.xlsx	Table
7	Binary	07-Article.pdf	.pdf	Table

Column1
%PDF-1.4
%◆◆◆◆
56 0 obj
<</Linearized 1/L 204554/O 58/E 70668/N 9/T 204130/H [461 242]>>
endobj
63 0 obj
<</DecodeParms<</Columns 4/Predictor 12>>/Filter/FlateDecode/ID[<D1
h◆bbd``b`Z5◆C◆`^S◆◆◆i◆D◆d&F◆◆ YF◆◆◆i◆ 1◆◆

Figure 9-6. *Result of the function for PDF files*

Excel.Workbook

Following the previous example, after calling the Excel files stored in a specific path by Folder.Content as binary values, to extract the tables in the excel files from binary values, Excel.Workbook can be used as follows:

```
Excel.Workbook(
        workbook as binary,
        optional useHeaders as any,
        optional delayTypes as nullable logical
            ) as table
```

Based on the syntax of this function, it takes these three arguments:

1. In the first argument, the name or address of the binary file is entered.

2. The second argument is optional and can be set to True or False for header settings.

3. The third input of this function is also optional and is used to determine the format of values in columns entering True or False.

In the previous example, entering the following formula instead of Csv.Document will get the result shown in Figure 9-7:

```
= Table.AddColumn(#"Removed Other Columns",

"Custom",

each Excel.Workbook([Content]))
```

	Content	AᴮC Name	AᴮC Extension	Custom
1	Binary	05-Inventory.csv	.csv	Error
2	Binary	05-Inventory.txt	.txt	Error
3	Binary	05-Inventory.xlsx	.xlsx	Table
4	Binary	06-Inventory.csv	.csv	Error
5	Binary	06-Inventory.txt	.txt	Error
6	Binary	06-Inventory.xlsx	.xlsx	Table
7	Binary	07-Article.pdf	.pdf	Error

Name	Data	Item	Kind	Hidden
06-Inventory	Table	06-Inventory	Sheet	FALSE

Figure 9-7. *Result of Excel.Workbook*

As you can see, for binary files with the XLSX extension, the result of this function is a new table containing values of that file, and for other file formats, the result of this function is an error.

Pdf.Tables

In the previous example, by using `Pdf.Tables` as follows, instead of `Excel.Workbook`, the values in the PDF file can be extracted:

```
Pdf.Tables(
        pdf as binary,
        optional options as nullable record
        ) as table
```

Based on the function syntax, this function receives these two inputs:

1. The name or address of the binary file for PDF is entered in the first input.

2. The second input of this function is optional, and settings related to the extracting values are entered.

According to the function explanations, by using the below formula in the previous example, instead of `Excel.Workbooks`, the values in the PDF file can be extracted:

```
= Table.AddColumn(#"Removed Other Columns",
"Custom", each Excel.Workbook([Content]))
```

The result is shown in Figure 9-8, where for binary files with the .pdf extension, the result of this function is equal to the new table containing the values stored in the PDF file. For other file types, the result of this function is an error.

	Content	AᵇC Name	AᵇC Extension	Custom
1	Binary	05-Inventory.csv	.csv	Error
2	Binary	05-Inventory.txt	.txt	Error
3	Binary	05-Inventory.xlsx	.xlsx	Error
4	Binary	06-Inventory.csv	.csv	Error
5	Binary	06-Inventory.txt	.txt	Error
6	Binary	06-Inventory.xlsx	.xlsx	Error
7	Binary	07-Article.pdf	.pdf	Table

Id	Name	Kind	Data
Page001	Page001	Page	Table
Page002	Page002	Page	Table
Page003	Page003	Page	Table
Page004	Page004	Page	Table
Page005	Page005	Page	Table
Page006	Page006	Page	Table
Page007	Page007	Page	Table
Table001	Table001 (Page 7)	Table	Table
Page008	Page008	Page	Table

Figure 9-8. *Extracting from PDF files*

Sql.Database

Sql.Database is defined in Power Query to call tables from a SQL database as follows:

```
Sql.Database(
server as text,
database as text,
optional options as nullable record
) as table
```

Based on the function syntax, this function receives three inputs:

1. The name of the server is entered as a text value in the first input.

2. The name of the database is entered as a text value in the second input.

3. The third input of this function is optional, and can be entered as `CreateNavigationProperties`, `NavigationPropertyNameGenerator`, `MaxDegreeOfParallelism`, `CommandTimeout`, `ConnectionTimeout`, `HierarchicalNavigation`, `MultiSubnetFailover`, `UnsafeTypeConversions`, `OmitSRID`, and `ssDatabaseFolding`.

Excel.CurrentWorkbook

`Excel.CurrentWorkbook` can be used in Excel for calling all tables in a current workbook into Power Query, like so:

`Excel.CurrentWorkbook() as table`

The `Excel.CurrentWorkbook` function is only used in Power Query in Excel. `Excel.CurrentWorkbook()` does not receive any input and always returns the tables stored in different sheets of the same Excel file where Power Query is active.

Summary

In this chapter, you embarked on a comprehensive journey through the realm of data extraction using Power Query's data source functions. The chapter highlighted the significance of accessing and unifying data from diverse sources to fuel informed decision-making.

The chapter commenced with an exploration of the fundamental concepts of data source functions. You saw how these functions enable Power Query to communicate with a range of data origins, from spreadsheets and databases to structured files. This foundational understanding set the stage for a deeper dive into data extraction techniques.

In the next chapter, which is the last one, some other functions for handling errors, conditions, and combining functions are presented.

CHAPTER 10

Other Functions

While Power Query's foundational functions empower you to navigate, shape, and aggregate data, there are moments when your data transformations demand an extra layer of sophistication. This is where the advanced functions come into play. They offer the ability to make nuanced decisions, handle exceptions gracefully, and craft custom expressions tailored to your specific needs.

Your journey through this chapter begins with the exploration of conditional logic, which is the art of asking questions of your data. Functions like IF introduce decision-making abilities into your data transformations. Whether it's filtering data based on specific conditions or dynamically altering calculations based on input, these functions empower you to craft custom, context-aware data flows.

But data isn't always pristine, and errors can creep in unexpectedly. This is where functions like TRY, OTHERWISE, and ERROR come to the rescue. You'll delve into the world of error handling, learning how to gracefully manage exceptions, replace missing values, and ensure that your data transformations continue even in the face of unforeseen challenges.

As you venture deeper into this chapter, you'll unveil the potential of LET, a function that might seem modest but holds the key to streamlining complex expressions. Learn how LET functions enhance readability and maintainability by breaking down intricate transformations into more digestible parts.

© Omid Motamedisedeh 2024
O. Motamedisedeh, *The Ultimate Guide to Functions in Power Query*,
https://doi.org/10.1007/978-1-4842-9754-4_10

Throughout your exploration, practical examples will illustrate the application of these advanced functions, bridging the gap between theory and real-world data scenarios. By the time you navigate through the intricacies of advanced functions in Power Query, you'll emerge with the ability to sculpt your data manipulations with a precision that goes beyond the surface. Your newfound mastery of conditional logic, error handling, and custom expressions will redefine the way you approach data transformation, enabling you to create solutions that elegantly adapt to the nuances of your data landscape.

if

The `if` in Power Query is very simple and is usually used within the `Table.AddColumns` function. This function is generally defined as follows:

> if (condition) then (result if the condition is true)
> else (result if the condition is false)

For example,

> =if a>2 then "Greater Than" else "Less Than"

In the above formula, the value of a is compared to the number 2. If the value of a is greater than 2, the result of the function will be "Greater Than" and if the number a is equal to or less than 2, the result of this formula will be "Less Than".

Consider TableC, as shown in Table 10-1.

Table 10-1. *TableC*

Row	Date	Product Name	Quantity
1	1/30/2023	A	17
2	1/31/2023	A	18
3	2/1/2023	C	10
4	2/1/2023	A	1
5	2/1/2023	B	6
6	2/2/2023	B	9
7	2/2/2023	A	6
8	2/3/2023	C	6
9	2/4/2023	B	10
10	2/4/2023	A	3
11	2/6/2023	C	18

The result of the following formula is equal to 11 (the number of rows) because TableC does not include duplicate rows:

```
= if Table.IsDistinct(TableC) then List.Count(TableC[Row]) else
"Table is not distinct"
```

However, if this table (TableC) contains duplicate rows, the result of this formula will be the text of "table is not distinct".

In another example, if the prices of product A, B, and C are respectively 10, 13, and 7 dollars, to add the sales column as a new column in TableC, the if function can be used inside Table.AddColumn as follows:

```
= Table.AddColumn(
        TableC,
        "Sales",
        each
        (if [Product Name]="A" then 10 else if [Product
        Name]="B" then 13 else 7)*[Quantity])
```

The result is shown in Table 10-2.

Table 10-2. *Result of if Function*

Row	Date	Product Name	Quantity	Sales
1	1/30/2023	A	17	170
2	1/31/2023	A	18	180
3	2/1/2023	C	10	70
4	2/1/2023	A	1	10
5	2/1/2023	B	6	78
6	2/2/2023	B	9	117
7	2/2/2023	A	6	60
8	2/3/2023	C	6	42
9	2/4/2023	B	10	130
10	2/4/2023	A	3	30
11	2/6/2023	C	18	126

Combining Conditions

To evaluate two or more conditions simultaneously, and and or can be used. For example, to identify the rows where the quantity of product A is greater than 10, two conditions can be defined as follows:

```
"Product Name" = "A" and "Quantity" > 10
```

When the word and is used between two conditions, the result will be true for the rows where the value of "A" is entered in the column of product name and the number registered in the quantity column is greater than 10. Therefore, the result of

```
= Table.AddColumn(
        TableC,
        "A and Greater than 10",
        each [Product Name]="A" and [Quantity]>10)
```

is equal to Table 10-3.

Table 10-3. *Combinations of Conditions by and*

Row	Date	Product Name	Quantity	A and Greater than 10
1	1/30/2023	A	17	TRUE
2	1/31/2023	A	18	TRUE
3	2/1/2023	C	10	FALSE
4	2/1/2023	A	1	FALSE
5	2/1/2023	B	6	FALSE
6	2/2/2023	B	9	FALSE
7	2/2/2023	A	6	FALSE
8	2/3/2023	C	6	FALSE
9	2/4/2023	B	10	FALSE
10	2/4/2023	A	3	FALSE
11	2/6/2023	C	18	FALSE

However, in the case where the word or is used between two conditions, the result will be true for rows where at least one of the two conditions (or both conditions) is met. In other words, for rows where the value "A" is recorded in the product name column or the number entered in the quantity column is greater than 10, the formula result will be true. Therefore, the result of

```
= Table.AddColumn(
        TableC,
        "A or Greater than 10",
        each [Product Name]="A" or [Quantity]>10)
```

is shown in Table 10-4.

Table 10-4. *Combinations of Conditions by or*

Row	Date	Product Name	Quantity	A or Greater than 10
1	1/30/2023	A	17	TRUE
2	1/31/2023	A	18	TRUE
3	2/1/2023	C	10	FALSE
4	2/1/2023	A	1	TRUE
5	2/1/2023	B	6	FALSE
6	2/2/2023	B	9	FALSE
7	2/2/2023	A	6	TRUE
8	2/3/2023	C	6	FALSE
9	2/4/2023	B	10	FALSE
10	2/4/2023	A	3	TRUE
11	2/6/2023	C	18	TRUE

It should be noted that in addition to the and and or functions, there is another function called not which is used to reverse the result of a condition. This function is always placed before the condition, and if the condition result is true, it is converted to false and vice versa. Therefore, when using the not in the last example (shown below), wherever the formula value in column A or Greater than 10 is equal to true, it is changed to false, and wherever the function value is equal to false, it is changed to true. See Table 10-5.

```
= Table.AddColumn(
      TableC,
      "A and Greater than 10",
      each not ([Product Name]="A" or [Quantity]>10))
      )
```

Table 10-5. *Application of not in Conditions*

Row	Date	Product Name	Quantity	A and Greater than 10
1	1/30/2023	A	17	FALSE
2	1/31/2023	A	18	FALSE
3	2/1/2023	C	10	TRUE
4	2/1/2023	A	1	FALSE
5	2/1/2023	B	6	TRUE
6	2/2/2023	B	9	TRUE
7	2/2/2023	A	6	FALSE
8	2/3/2023	C	6	TRUE
9	2/4/2023	B	10	TRUE
10	2/4/2023	A	3	FALSE
11	2/6/2023	C	18	FALSE

The try Function

The try function is used to handle errors in Power Query and can be used to prevent showing errors. For example, if the following formula is entered in Power Query, the result will be equal to the number 2. (The data format is converted from text to number.)

=Number.From("2")

However, using Number.From for the text "A" as follows will result in an error:

=Number.From("A")

In this case, the calculation stops due to the error, and the result shown in Figure 10-1 is obtained.

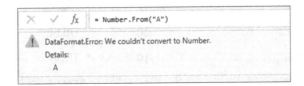

Figure 10-1. *Error result*

Therefore, to handle these conditions, the try function is used. The result of this function is equal to a record with two fields in the form of [HasError=False, Value=2].

=try Number.From("2")

Using this function in a case where the result of the function is an error (as in the following example), the function result will contain a record that specifies the cause of the error:

=try Number.From("A")

For the above function, the result is equal to the following record:

```
[HasError=True, Error=
        [Reason= "DataFormat.Error",
        Message="We couldn't convert to Number.",
        Detail="A",
        Message.Format= "We couldn't convert to Number.",
        Message.Parameters= null]]
```

As you can see, the first field of the output specifies that the formula result is an error, and the second field (Error) provides additional information about the reason for the error and the message displayed to the user.

In a more complete form of the try function, it can be used with the otherwise operator as follows:

```
= try Number.From("2") otherwise " Wrong Input "
```

In this case, the function tries to calculate Number.From("2") and display its result in the output. If the result of the formula Number.From("2") is an error, the expression " Wrong Input " will be displayed in the output. In other cases, the result of the formula will be displayed in the output.

Therefore, the result of the following formula is equal to the number 2:

```
= try Number.From("2") otherwise " Wrong Input "
```

And the result of the following formula is equal to the expression "Wrong Input":

```
= try Number.From("A") otherwise "Wrong Input"
```

The let-in Command

In Power Query, the cleaning and transformation operations (such as merging tables, deleting columns, and adding new columns) are commonly more complex than stating one function in a single step.

To simplify the process, this function is used to divide the whole command into several lines by defining new variables. For example, in the following formula, this function is used to define variables A and B with the value of 2 and 3, and finally, the variable C is defined; its value equals A*B, and its value (6) is shown as the result of all steps.

```
let
    A=2,
    B=3,
    C=A*B
in
    C
```

As you can see, the commands start with the let expression, followed by the variable name and its value after the equal sign. The variable name can include spaces (e.g., A A), which should be defined in double quotes after the # sign, as in #"A A". Each command ends with a comma (except the last one before the in expression) and is followed by the next variable definition. In each command, the user can refer to the variables defined in other commands (the previous or next one). This function ends with the keyword in and then the name of variable you want to show as the function output is mentioned.

The following is an example of the let-in function in Power Query:

```
let
    Table = Table.FromColumns(
            {{1,2,3,4,5,6,7,8,9,10,11},
```

```
    {44956,44957,44958,44958,44958,44959,44959,44960,
    44961,44961,44963},
    {"A","A","C","A","B","B","A","C","B","A","C"},
    {17,18,10,1,6,9,6,6,10,3,18}},
    {"Row" ,"Date","Product Name","Quantity"}),
Changed_Type_ColumnDate = Table.TransformColumnTypes
(Table,{{"Date", type date}}),
Removed_Column_Row = Table.RemoveColumns
(Changed_Type_ColumnDate,{"Row"}),
Added_Column_Sales = Table.AddColumn(Removed_Column_Row,
"Sale", each [Quantity]*10)
in

Added_Column_Sales
```

In this command, initially the variable named table is defined, and the result is shown in Table 10-6.

Table 10-6. *First Step: Define the Table*

Row	Date	Product Name	Quantity
1	44956	A	17
2	44957	A	18
3	44958	C	10
4	44958	A	1
5	44958	B	6
6	44959	B	9
7	44959	A	6
8	44960	C	6
9	44961	B	10
10	44961	A	3
11	44963	C	18

In the next step, which is named Changed_Type_ColumnDate, the format of the Date column is changed to date by using Table. TransformColumnTypes. The result of this step is shown in Table 10-7.

Table 10-7. *Second Step: Change the Data Type*

Row	Date	Product Name	Quantity
1	1/30/2023	A	17
2	1/31/2023	A	18
3	2/1/2023	C	10
4	2/1/2023	A	1
5	2/1/2023	B	6
6	2/2/2023	B	9
7	2/2/2023	A	6
8	2/3/2023	C	6
9	2/4/2023	B	10
10	2/4/2023	A	3
11	2/6/2023	C	18

In the next step, which is titled Removed_Column_Row, the column with the name of Row is removed from the previous table using the Remove. TableColumns function. The result is shown in Table 10-8.

Table 10-8. *Third Step: Remove the Row Column*

Date	Product Name	Quantity
1/30/2023	A	17
1/31/2023	A	18
2/1/2023	C	10
2/1/2023	A	1
2/1/2023	B	6
2/2/2023	B	9
2/2/2023	A	6
2/3/2023	C	6
2/4/2023	B	10
2/4/2023	A	3
2/6/2023	C	18

Finally, in the last step, named Added_Column_Sales, a new column named Sales is added to the previous table. See Table 10-9.

Table 10-9. *Fourth Step: Add a New Column*

Date	Product Name	Quantity	Sales
1/30/2023	A	17	170
1/31/2023	A	18	180
2/1/2023	C	10	100
2/1/2023	A	1	10
2/1/2023	B	6	60
2/2/2023	B	9	90
2/2/2023	A	6	60
2/3/2023	C	6	60
2/4/2023	B	10	100
2/4/2023	A	3	30
2/6/2023	C	18	180

So, by using let-in, several actions have been done on a table in different steps.

It should be noted that instead of the let-in command, records can also be used to divide calculations into multiple steps. For example, [A=2, B=3, C=A*B][C] can be used to calculate the C in three steps.

The following points should be considered in the use of Power Query commands:

1. **Case sensitivity**: As well as function names, the names of variables are also case-sensitive.

2. **Variable addressing**: The order of defining variables in the let-in command is not important, and you can reference previous or next variables in the formula for each variable (since causing a loop).

3. **Unique variable names**: In the let-in command, the name of variables should be unique.

4. **Commenting**: To enter a comment at the end of a command, it can be entered after the // sign. To enter the comment in multiple lines, it should be put between the /* and */ signs. The comments are only visible in the Power Query editor and will not be displayed in the formula bar.

5. **Writing code in multiple lines**: Each command line in the M language should end with a semicolon. So, a long command can easily be entered in multiple lines, starting with the variable name and ending with a semicolon.

6. **Sensitivity to value format**: As mentioned, the type of variable is very important in the M language, and each function can be applied to a specific type of value.

Defining a New Function

In addition to the functions taught in this book, it is possible to define a new function in Power Query. To create a function in Power Query, first the variable names are listed in parentheses, followed by the symbol =>, as the function symbol. Then the desired formula is entered. The following is an example of a simple function that can add 1 to numerical values:

$$(X) => X+1$$

In the above formula, parameter x is the input of defined function and its output is equal to X+1.

In another example, the following function receives two parameters, X and Y, as input and displays their product in the output:

$$(X,Y) => X*Y$$

Since the required functions in practical examples are usually more complex than the previous example and need to be write in multiple lines, you can usually use the let command to divide the function calculation section into several lines, as in the following formula:

```
(x)=>
    let
        a=x+1,
        b=a*x,
        c= if b > 10 then b*2 else b-2
    in
    c
```

In this function, variable x is the input and the output is calculated in three stages. In the first stage, the value of x is added to the number 1. In the second stage, the number x is multiplied by the value obtained from the previous stage (a). Finally, based on the value obtained in the previous stage, if the result is greater than 10, it is multiplied by 2 and displayed in the output, and if the result is smaller than 10, the obtained number is subtracted by 2 and displayed in the output.

Based on the function explanation, let's discuss a few examples of creating a new function in Excel. See Figure 10-2.

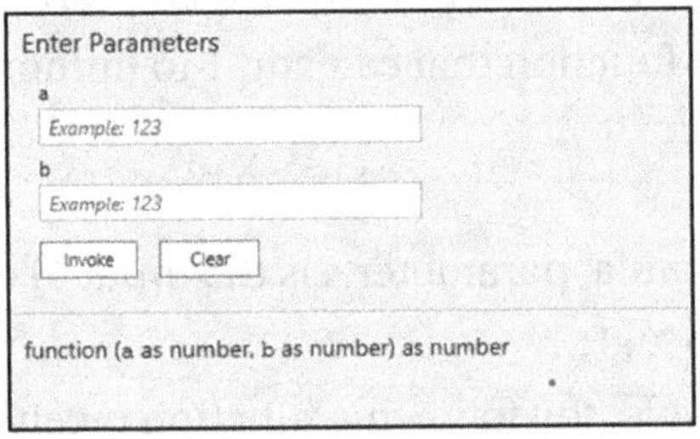

Figure 10-2. Tax evaluation

- Tax calculation function:

  In this example, we want to create a new function in Power Query that takes a number as the input and calculates the amount of tax based on its value. If the number is less than 100, the tax rate is 0%, and if the number is greater than 100, the tax rate is 10%.

  So the new function can be defined as follows:

  (x) => if x<100 then 0 else 0.1*x

- Sum of numbers between a and b:

  Say you want to define a new function that takes two numbers, a, and b, as the input and displays the sum of integer numbers between a and b in the output.

  To solve this problem, you need to create all the integers between a and b and then add them up. To do this, you can use the following formula to create a new function:

376

(a,b) => List.Sum({a..b})

In this case, if the numbers 1 and 5 are entered instead of a and b, the result of the function is 15. However, if the number 1.1 is entered instead of 1 in parameter a, the result is an error. Let's change the above formula to the following formula:

(a,b) => List.Sum({Number.RoundUp(a)..Number. RoundDown(b)})

In this case, both parameter a and parameter b are first converted to integers and then are used in the calculations.

In the above definition, the format of the functions' inputs and output are not specified, so the user can enter any value. The formula result will be an error if text values are entered. See Figure 10-3.

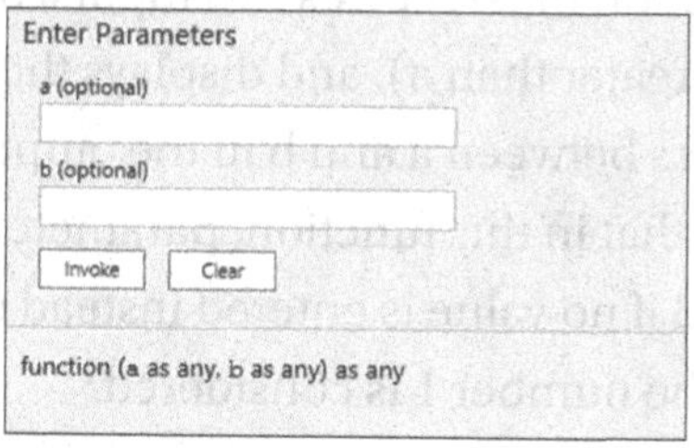

Figure 10-3. Function inputs

However, if you want to define the format of the function's inputs and output, you can specify them, as follows:

(an as number,b as number) as number =>
List.Sum({Number.RoundUp(a)..Number.
RoundDown(b)})

As you can see in Figure 10-4, here the types of
function inputs and outputs are specified.

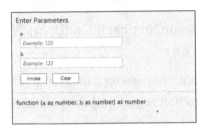

Figure 10-4. *Function inputs with specific format*

- Sum of numbers between b and a with optional input:

  Similar to the previous example, here you want to
  define a function that receives two inputs, b and a
  (where b is greater than a), and displays the sum
  of all numbers between a and b in the output. The
  difference is that in this function, parameter a is
  optional, and if no value is entered instead of this
  parameter, the number 1 is considered.

  To do this, you can define the optional input in a
  new function as "optional x", so the new function is
  defined as follows:

  (b as number, optional a as number) as number =>
  List.Sum({Number.RoundUp(if a=null then 1 else
  a)..Number.RoundDown(b)})

In this case, since parameter a is defined as optional, parameter b will be mandatory, and the user will be faced with the form in Figure 10-5 when entering data.

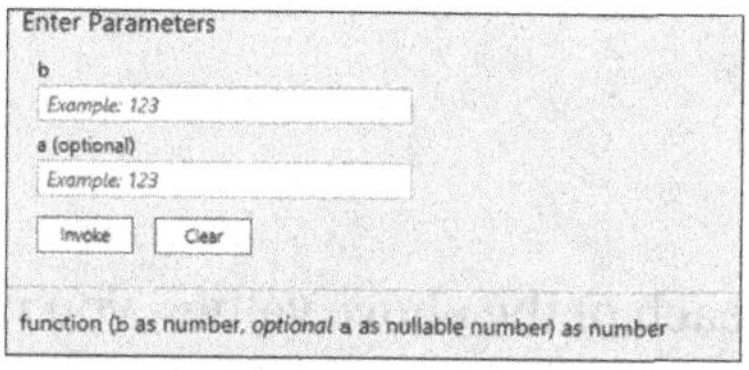

Figure 10-5. *Definition of optional input*

- Nth number in a Fibonacci sequence:

In this example, you want to write a function that takes an integer (n) as the input and displays the nth number from the Fibonacci sequence in the output. (The Fibonacci sequence is {1,1,2,3,5,8,13, ...} and each number is obtained by adding the two previous numbers.) To solve this problem, you need to be familiar with recursive functions. Recursive functions are functions in which the function name is used again in the formula based on the conditions.

Before solving this problem, let's assume that you name the fifth number from the Fibonacci sequence as a5 and want to calculate it. To do this, according to the general formula of the Fibonacci function, the value of a5 is calculated as follows:

a5 = a4 + a3

Therefore, to calculate the value of a5 in the Fibonacci sequence, you need to use the definition of the Fibonacci sequence again and calculate the values of a4 and a3, which are equal to the following values:

a4 = a3 + a2

a3 = a2 + a1

To calculate each of the above values, you need to use the definition of the Fibonacci sequence again and calculate the lower values, and this process continues until you reach the two values a1 and a0. Therefore, the Fibonacci calculation formula needs to be defined recursively.

To do this, first change the query name to fibo and use the following to obtain the nth value in the Fibonacci sequence:

(n) => if n<=1 then 1 else fibo(n-1)+fibo(n-2)

Using Defined Function in Other Queries

After creating a new function in Power Query, the query name can be changed from the query settings (right window). After defining the desired name for the function, like other functions, the new function can be used in advanced calculations of other queries in the same power query file. See Figure 10-6.

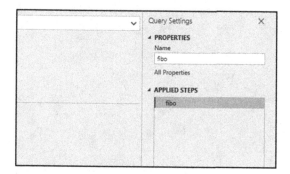

Figure 10-6. *Changing a function's name*

Index

A, B

Binary values, 30, 350, 353

C

Columns names, 349
  Table.ColumnNames, 246
  Table.ColumnsOfType, 250, 251
  Table.DemoteHeaders, 246, 247
  Table.HasColumns, 249–251
  Table.PrefixColumns, 251, 252
  Table.PromoteHeaders, 247–249
  Table.RenameColumns,
    252, 253
Combinations of
  conditions, 363–367
Combining tables
  Table.Combine, 303–308
  Table.Join, 308–316
  Table.NestedJoin, 317–320
Constant values, 37, 38
Csv.Document, 349–353

D

Data conversion
  data formats, 32
  date and time format, 35

number format, 33, 34
record format, 35, 36
text, 79–81
text format, 34, 35
Data sources
  Csv.Document, 349–353
  Excel.CurrentWorkbook, 357
  Excel.Workbook, 353–355
  Folder.Contents, 348, 349
  functions, 347
  Pdf.Tables, 355, 356
  Power Query, 347
  Sql.Database, 356, 357
Data types, 46, 99, 157, 159,
  179, 345
  binary value, 30
  function, 31
  initial characters, 23
  list, 30
  logical values, 25
  null value, 25
  numbers, 26, 27
  in Power Query, 24, 25
  record, 31
  samples, 24
  table, 31
  text, 30
  time and date, 27–30

© Omid Motamedisedeh 2024
O. Motamedisedeh, *The Ultimate Guide to Functions in Power Query*,
https://doi.org/10.1007/978-1-4842-9754-4

S

T, U, V, W, X, Y, Z

Printed in the United States
by Baker & Taylor Publisher Services